The twentieth century has seen biology come of age as a conceptual and quantitative science. Major functional phenomena rather than catalogues of animals and plants comprise the core of MODERN BIOLOGY; such heretofore seemingly unrelated fields as cytology, biochemistry, and genetics are now being unified into a common framework at the molecular level.

The purpose of this Series is to introduce the beginning student in college biology—as well as the gifted high school student and all interested readers—both to the concepts unifying the fields of biology and to the diversity of facts that give the entire field its unique texture. Each book in the Series is an introduction to one of the major foundation stones in the mosaic. Taken together, they provide an integration of the general and the comparative, the cellular and the organismic, the animal and the plant, the structural and the functional—in sum, a solid overview of the dynamic science that is MODERN BIOLOGY.

MODERN BIOLOGY SERIES

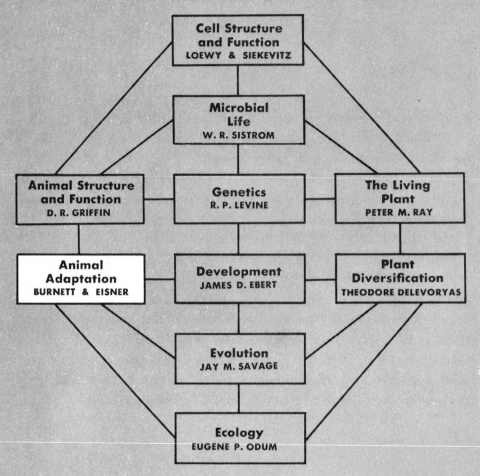

Cell Structure and Function
LOEWY & SIEKEVITZ

Microbial Life
W. R. SISTROM

Animal Structure and Function
D. R. GRIFFIN

Genetics
R. P. LEVINE

The Living Plant
PETER M. RAY

Animal Adaptation
BURNETT & EISNER

Development
JAMES D. EBERT

Plant Diversification
THEODORE DELEVORYAS

Evolution
JAY M. SAVAGE

Ecology
EUGENE P. ODUM

HOLT, RINEHART AND WINSTON

NEW YORK · CHICAGO · SAN FRANCISCO · TORONTO · LONDON

ANIMAL

ADAPTATION

ALLISON L. BURNETT

WESTERN RESERVE UNIVERSITY

THOMAS EISNER

CORNELL UNIVERSITY

PREFACE

Adaptation is perhaps the most basic concept in biology. It is also very largely a self-evident concept: organisms are surviving because they are adapted, and they are adapted because they are surviving. In one sense, therefore, our book is no more than an elaboration of the obvious. We have not attempted to present a broadly encompassing treatment of the subject, nor do we feel that the particular topics selected are especially profound ones. Our goal has been merely to convey some feeling for the ways in which biologists think about their organisms of choice. The selection of a mosquito as our frame of reference was purely incidental.

We have consciously avoided dealing with the genetic basis of adaptation. For a discussion of this important topic the reader is referred to *Evolution* and *Genetics* in this series.

Several friends have been helpful and offered suggestions along the way. In particular we thank Rosalind Alsop, W. L. Brown, Jr., J. S. Edwards, H. E. Evans, Fotis Kafatos, W. T. Keeton, Michael Locke, Bruce Wallace, and E. O. Wilson.

Cleveland, Ohio
Ithaca, New York
November, 1963

A.L.B.
T.E.

v

CONTENTS

A

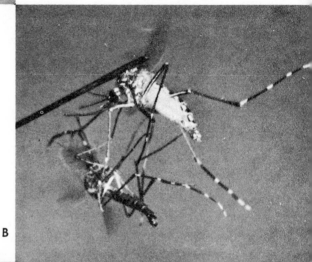

B

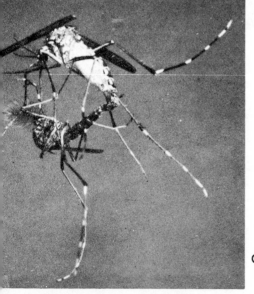

A male of the mosquito *Aedes aegypti*, attracted to the sound emitted by the beating wings of a tethered female, flies toward her (A), seizes her from beneath (B), and mates with her (C).

C

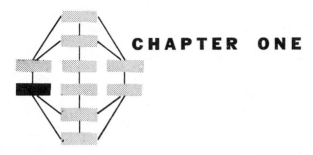

CHAPTER ONE

A

CASE

STUDY In 1878, Hiram Maxim made a remarkable discovery. Maxim, an engineer, had just installed a lighting apparatus for a hotel in northern New York. He noticed that soon after a dynamo that powered one of his lamps was turned on, the lamp became covered with mosquitoes trying to enter the box, which was emitting a peculiar hum. The fact that mosquitoes were attracted to the lamp box was in itself an interesting phenomenon, but what whetted Maxim's imagination was that all of the mosquitoes were males.

What properties of a lamp box could possibly be of interest to a male mosquito? Two obvious possibilities were that the box emitted an odor similar to that of the male mosquitoes' natural food, or that the steady sound produced by the lamp box was somehow attractive to male mosquitoes. Maxim began by testing the second possibility—sound. Reasoning that perhaps the tone of the box mimicked in some manner the sound produced by a female mosquito, Maxim struck a tuning fork that produced a hum similar to that of a female mosquito in flight. He had his answer almost immediately, for he found that male mosquitoes in the vicinity would turn in mid-air and fly toward the tuning fork (Fig. 1–1).

Maxim was not satisfied with this single experiment. He wished to discover the mechanism by which the male mosquito was able to hear the female, since the animal possesses no obvious auditory organ. By careful, close observation of the male animal, he discovered two small hair-covered antennae projecting from the head. From this observation he reasoned: "It then occurred to me that the two little feathers [antennae] on the head of the male mosquito acted as ears, that they vibrated in unison with the music of the lamp, and as the pitch of the note was almost identical with the buzzing of the female mosquito, the male took the music to be the buzzing of the female."

1

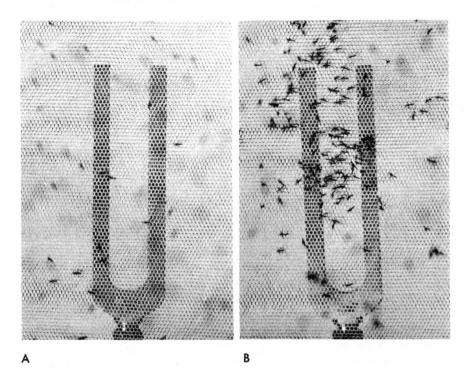

A   **B**

Fig. 1-1. Response of male *Aedes* to a tuning fork. At (A) the fork is silent; at (B) it is emitting sound and attracting males. (Photographs courtesy of Dr. E. R. Willis.)

More sophisticated experiments than Maxim's were carried out later on *Aedes aegypti*, the mosquito that has had a notorious role in man's history as the carrier of the dreaded yellow fever virus. Maxim's hypothesis turned out to be entirely correct. On any warm summer day, amid innumerable sounds around them, male *Aedes* are searching out particular sounds emitted within a specific frequency range. Homing in on the sound, the male locates the female and ultimately succeeds in overcoming a problem faced by hosts of animals that engage in sexual reproduction—that of introducing sperm into the female genital system.

A biologist after reading this isolated observation of Maxim's would immediately be bombarded by a number of questions. What is the physiological basis of the hearing mechanism? How does the sound produced by the female in flight differ from that of the male or from different species of mosquitoes? Can mating occur without the beckoning wing call of the female? Is the response to the call instinctive or is it learned? Some of the answers are known; others are not.

Hosts of scientists have devoted years of research time to *Aedes;* their combined efforts have revealed to us, some 85 years after Maxim's report, dozens of exciting and elegant adaptations that have contributed to the survival of this species.

The purpose of this text is to examine the concept of *adaptation*. The authors believe that a neat, well-pruned definition of adaptation fails to convey to the reader a feeling for what adaptation is, just as a definition of an easy chair fails to describe the satisfaction one feels when one sinks his tired body into it. To gain an appreciation of adaptation one must live with an organism for a long period of time. The choice of the organism is purely incidental; we might choose a lion, alligator, puppy, or kangaroo. The important thing is to observe how the animal lives, where it lives, how it is put together, and how its structural components function—in short, how it is fit for survival in the world of today. As we examine the collective processes that contribute to the animal's survival, we witness adaptive events that are precisely geared to fulfill the basic requisites of life. So let us spend some time with this animal, *Aedes aegypti,* the yellow fever mosquito.

LIFE CYCLE

We will begin at the beginning. The animal whose life cycle we will examine has not yet been conceived. Part of it is contained in the sperm of a male *Aedes* that is on wing searching for its mate, the female in whose ovaries the egg cells are forming. The sperm and the egg must fuse. We began with a discussion of the mechanism through which *Aedes* locates its mate. Let us now examine this process in more detail.

When the male mosquito first emerges from the pupal shell in which it developed, it is incapable of fertilizing the female. The genital apparatus must first undergo a 180° rotation before sexual competence is achieved, and this process is not completed until 24 hours after emergence. By means of a truly elegant adaptation the male is maintained deaf during this period and is thereby prevented from fruitlessly expending energy in searching for a female when he is still sexually incompetent.

It was mentioned previously that the antennae of the male are covered with long hairs. When sounds of the proper frequency impinge upon the antennae, they vibrate in unison. These vibrations are transmitted to large aggregates of sensory cells at the base of the antennae (Fig. 1–2). These sensory cells translate the vibrations into the language of the nervous system —that is, into nerve impulses. A volley of impulses passes to the brain and then to the proper muscles that trigger the flight machinery into action. The male flies to the female. At the time of adult emergence, however, the antennal hairs lie recumbent upon the shaft of the antenna. Without an erect set of hairs the antenna is far less responsive to sound, for the hairs provide it with an amplifier system. Thus during its first 24 hours the male

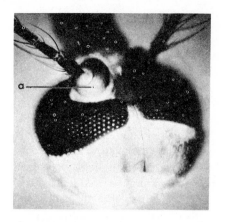 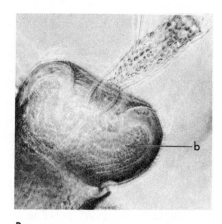

A   **B**

Fig. 1-2. A: Head of male *Aedes* showing, on the left antenna, the swollen segment, a, that houses the receptor cells that sense the antennal vibrations. This swollen segment is shown in cross section at (B), revealing the densely packed cells within it, b.

is deaf and nonresponsive to the buzz of the female. Only later, when the genital apparatus is properly oriented, and the male capable of fertilization, do the hairs become erect for the reception of the female signal (Fig. 1–3).

The beauty of this mechanism lies in the fact that two completely separate but necessarily interdependent events are synchronized to the obvious advantage of the animal. If the encounters between the sexes were solely a matter of chance, then perpetuation of the species might be seriously jeopardized. The mosquito possesses an excellent mechanism that not only maximizes the frequency of encounters but prevents useless ones from occurring.

Once the female mosquito has been located by the male, copulation begins, usually taking place in mid-air. The male animal flies to the female, seizes her, and orients himself beneath her in such a manner that the abdomens face one another with their tips in contact (Frontispiece). Then by means of an intromittent organ the male injects sperm directly into the female genital tract. This entire process is usually completed on the wing and lasts only a few seconds. Occasionally, both partners tumble to the ground after the male has seized the female and copulation takes place wherever they happen to land. By mating in flight they minimize the chance of tumbling into a potentially hazardous environment.

At this point the female assumes the dominant role in perpetuating the species. After copulation she must secure a blood meal from a vertebrate; if she fails, her eggs will not develop. *Aedes aegypti* usually lives close to human habitations. Although the female may feed upon rabbits and guinea pigs in the laboratory, and upon bats in nature, man is the principal source of its blood meal. The male mosquito never feeds upon blood, but upon

Fig. 1-3. A: Head of freshly emerged "deaf" male, with antennal hairs recumbent against shaft. B: Head of mature male with typical feathery antennae. a, antenna; b, maxillary palp; c, proboscis.

sugary fluids obtained from plants. In addition to her blood meal, the female will also feed upon the liquid exudates of flowers.

Although many annoyed humans may think otherwise, the mosquito's problem of obtaining blood from a human host is by no means an easy one. First, the mosquito is not a strong flier. Second, it must penetrate through a thick epidermis and reach the blood stream of an animal that can bring about its annihilation with a single slap of the hand. Third, after cutting through the skin of the host, it must gorge itself with more than its own weight within a period of from two to five minutes (Fig. 1–4).

Aedes is primarily a diurnal species and it usually approaches the host from the shady side. The mosquito has been guided to its blood meal mainly by sight, but there is some evidence that the warm currents of air in the immediate vicinity of the host as well as the exhaled carbon dioxide and some other chemicals emanating from the host may also serve as attractants. Although a mosquito that flies around a bedroom at night can be annoyingly audible, this buzz is not so obvious in diurnal species whose approach is no less silent but whose drone is likely to be masked by competing sounds, including the voice of the host itself. The mosquito alights so gently that its immediate impact on the skin is rarely felt. The animal does not tramp

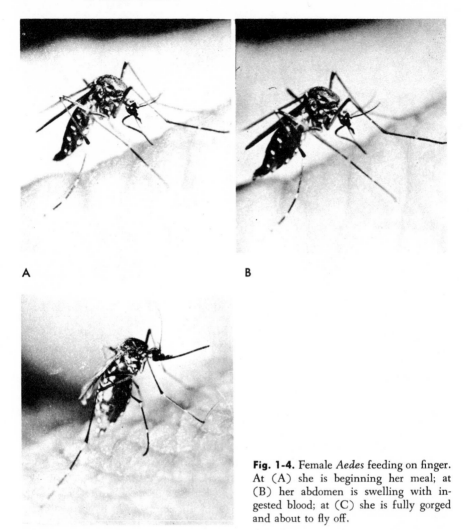

A

B

Fig. 1-4. Female *Aedes* feeding on finger. At (A) she is beginning her meal; at (B) her abdomen is swelling with ingested blood; at (C) she is fully gorged and about to fly off.

C

over the skin in search of a tender, thin layer, but begins to puncture almost immediately after landing.

The mouth parts of the mosquito (Fig. 1–5) are highly modified and include four long, very slender scalpels that cut cleanly and swiftly through the skin. Another mouth part forms a food channel through which the blood of the host is sucked into the mouth in a manner somewhat analogous to sipping through a straw. It would be wrong to state that the bite of the mosquito is completely painless, but as anyone who sits on an unscreened porch during a warm summer evening can testify, many mosquitoes manage

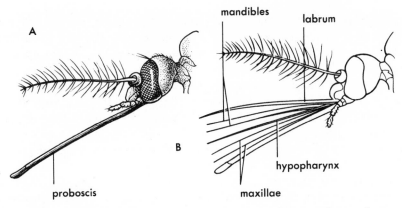

Fig. 1-5. A: Head of female in lateral view. B: Same, with mouth parts separated from the proboscis that normally sheathes them. The labrum encloses the canal through which food is aspirated. The mandibles and maxillae form the "scalpels" that cut through the skin. The hypopharynx is hollow, and serves to inject saliva into the wound. (After R. E. Snodgrass.)

to get away unnoticed with a full blood meal. The major annoyance to most people occurs not during the bite, but immediately after, when the area near the wound begins to swell and itch.

As a result of this single blood meal, *Aedes* ensures that its eggs will go on to complete their development. The final task faced by the parent is that of finding a proper place to deposit the eggs, one in which the off-spring stand a chance for survival. The search for the oviposition site begins two to four days after the blood meal. The female is now ready to lay from 100 to 120 eggs in a specific environment.

Oviposition always occurs at a water site. Why a terrestrial creature that is adapted to life on land goes into water for part of its life is a question worth pondering, and we shall have more to say about it later. For the present, it suffices to say that the female will be attracted to such diverse water sources as cracks in masonry, uncovered cisterns, traps of drains, water closets that are temporarily out of use, bamboo stumps, and tree holes. In these small bodies of water the mosquito will pass its larval and pupal existence.

The many species of mosquitoes other than *Aedes* that breed in ponds, marshes, and other large bodies of water ordinarily lay their eggs on the surface. However, in small bodies of water there is a greater threat of desiccation, which would be devastating to the larvae. *Aedes* possesses an adaptive mechanism that guards against this threat. Instead of laying the eggs directly on the water surface, the female deposits them by means of a sticky adhesive pad just above the water line. The eggs will not hatch until the water level rises to meet them. This ensures that the young will hatch into a medium that is rising in level rather than drying out. This type of oviposition has another major advantage that is much more subtle and possibly more important than that already mentioned. We will discuss this in the next chapter, leaving the reader an opportunity to speculate for himself.

The female does not lay her entire batch of eggs in one location so that a single calamity can undo her labor of the past four days. Instead, she lands near the water's edge, dips her abdominal tip to the substratum, and deposits only a few eggs at a time. Without moving her legs, she extends her abdomen in another direction and repeats this procedure. After depositing a few clusters, she moves a short distance and repeats the operation. By distributing her eggs in several clusters, often near different water sources, the female not only minimizes the possibility of their simultaneous destruction, but prevents the subsequent overcrowding of her offspring in an environment of limited food supply.

After the female has deposited the eggs she has no further role in bringing about the successful development of her offspring. Although she may mate several times over the next two or three months, taking several blood meals and laying over 700 eggs, she will never have the reproductive vigor she possessed after her first copulation. Subsequent matings always result in the production of fewer and fewer eggs.

The act of depositing an egg is a simple one, but it must be preceded by a series of precisely timed events, such as locating a mate, copulating, securing a blood meal, and locating a favorable oviposition site. Furthermore, we have mentioned only a few of the outstanding behavioral and structural adaptations that accompany the reproductive phenomenon. If we knew all there is to know concerning this phenomenon, down to the molecular level, our text would fill dozens of volumes, and in its own right one adaptation would be no less important to successful oviposition than another.

Within a few hours, the adhesive pad on the egg dries into a hard cement that fixes the egg firmly in position. Within the egg an embryo is developing. The animal is soon to begin life in an environment vastly different from the terrestrial one. What food materials can be found in artificial containers, such as cracks in masonry? How does an animal whose parent is adapted to breathe air survive in water that contains 20 times less oxygen per unit volume? Since the wings of the adult would hardly function as locomotory organs in an aquatic larva, how then does the larva get about? And finally, how does the larva living in water succeed in its transformation into a winged terrestrial adult? To attack such questions we must scrutinize the behavioral and structural adaptations of this curious aquatic stage that occurs in the life of every mosquito.

For the first 24 hours after oviposition, the egg must be moist to ensure the development of the embryo. Since oviposition occurs on surfaces just above the water level, this critical requirement for moisture is usually met.

After the initial moist phase the egg can withstand dryness for several months. During this time the embryo is in a dormant state known as diapause, and its metabolism is at a minimal level. However, the moment the water level rises and contacts the egg, diapause is broken, and within minutes the young larva is ready to emerge. As if in anticipation of hatching, the embryo is provided with a hard, thorn-shaped structure that projects from its head.

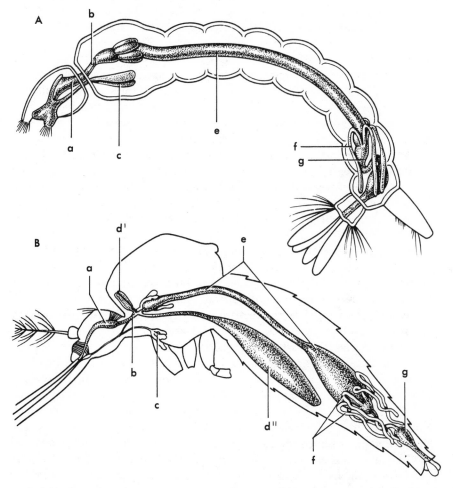

Fig. 1-6. Digestive tract of larva (A) and adult (B). The pharynx, a, and esophagus, b, constitute the fore-gut. Salivary glands, c, open just in front of the pharynx. In the adult the fore-gut has two small dorsal diverticuli, d', and a large ventral one d''. Behind the fore-gut is the mid-gut, e, which in the larva has an anterior ring of oblong diverticular pouches. At the junction of the mid-gut and hind-gut are the excretory Malpighian tubules (f). The terminal portion of the hind-gut is the rectum, g. (Modified from R. E. Snodgrass.)

This temporary structure, known as the egg breaker, apparently initiates the crack along the shell through which the larva will emerge. Emergence is also aided by an active swallowing of water; this increases the animal's volume and causes the crack to widen. When the crack expands sufficiently, the larva emerges and promptly swims to the surface by active side-lashing movements of its body.

If we were to peer through the surface film we would see the larva hanging upside down (Fig. 1–8) with only the small tube (siphon) at the tip of its abdomen making contact with the surface. Except for the siphon and the head, which are almost black, the larva is completely white and is covered with a transparent cuticle. As it hangs from the surface film, the larva is sometimes seen to move slowly just beneath the surface, although it contains no legs and its body is motionless. Various questions immediately arise from these routine observations. How does an animal that hangs from the surface only by the siphon obtain oxygen? How does an animal with no legs glide along the surface film? What purpose does gliding serve?

The answer to the first question is simple. If detergent is added to the water, the surface tension is reduced, making it impossible for the larva to maintain its attachment; the animal sinks and dies. It has, in fact, drowned. Closer examination of the siphon shows that at its tip there are two round openings (Fig. 1–9B). These lead inward into two big air-filled tubes (tracheal trunks) that course the entire length of the larva, giving off branches and subbranches that penetrate all the various tissues of the animal (Fig. 1–10). This ramified system of air-filled vessels (*tracheae*) forms the respiratory system of the animal. The larva breathes air, and in order to get it must bring the tip of its siphon to the surface. In this respect the larva is no better adapted to life in water than is a seal, which must also surface periodically for air.

It would seem at first that an aquatic form that is restricted to the surface because of its need for air but nevertheless must feed on materials below the surface is in an awkward predicament. The hatched larva has been formed at the expense of an energy reserve that was present in the original egg. If the larva is to grow to adulthood, it must now become an active feeder. But on what can it feed as it hangs from the surface?

A prominent source of organic food in the larval habitat is bacteria and other small particulate matter suspended in the water. The larva feeds by devouring millions of bacteria, accomplishing this without swallowing hundreds of mouthfulls of water into the intestine. The gliding motion of the larva is an indication of the animal's grazing activity as it moves from one food-laden area to another.

Both the gliding motion and the food intake depend upon the same structural components. Around the mouth of the animal there are two small brushes, densely covered with hairs (Figs. 1–7 and 1–8). During feeding,

A

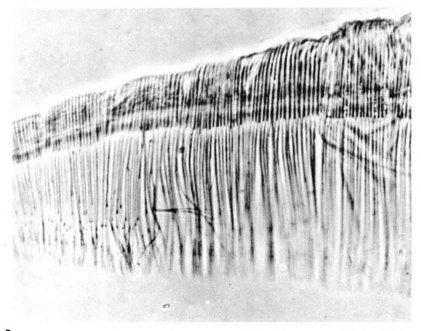

B

Fig. 1-7. A: Isolated food brush of larva (see also Fig. 1-13A). B: Highly enlarged portion of one of the combs that retain particulate solids in the pharyngeal filter of the larva.

the brushes beat rapidly in a circular, scooping motion that sets up currents of water directed toward the mouth. Particulate material in the water becomes trapped in the hairs and is eventually passed into the mouth. Just behind the mouth is an expanded region of the digestive system, the pharynx (Fig. 1–6A). As the particles are passed into the pharynx, water, as the carrier, is unavoidably also admitted. Here in the pharynx, a most interesting water-eliminating mechanism comes into action. After the pharynx becomes filled with water and food materials, muscles around the pharynx contract, and water is regurgitated. This contraction does not completely collapse the pharynx; two small marginal canals remain open. These canals are lined with tiny bristles that strain out the suspended solids while water is being regurgitated (Fig. 1–7B). Through continued pharyngeal action, particles accumulate until they form a small clump, or bolus. Eventually, by a power-ful swallowing action, the entire bolus is passed back into the major part of the gut, clearing the pharyngeal canals. Thus, the mosquito's dependence on the surface film does not handicap its feeding efforts. This type of food intake is known as filter feeding, and is practiced also by the largest animal alive, the blue whale, which strains small shrimplike creatures from the ocean.

The question of locomotion has already been answered. The action of the food brushes sweeping water into the mouth produces a force sufficient to propel the animal slowly from one feeding ground to another. Multiplicity of function is not unusual, and the mosquito's mouth parts are but one example of how anatomical fitness is not necessarily gauged to fulfill a single adaptive need. Consider your own hand.

Actually the larva does not spend all of its time at the surface. A sudden change in light intensity or vibration will instantly cause it to wiggle to the bottom. These reactions are obviously of defensive significance. But the larva may also dive on its own initiative, and it is not uncommon to find one browsing on submerged surfaces. The brushes create currents that loosen particles from the surfaces and direct them to the mouth. Young larvae can withstand submersion for one or even several days (why might this be?). Older ones resurface frequently, and die within hours if prevented from doing so.

During the next six days the continuously feeding larva will grow from two millimeters to over seven millimeters in length. This is the only time during its lifetime that *Aedes* will grow in size, and one may well ponder the question of why growth is limited to a single transient stage in the animal's existence. Certainly this is not the only feeding period in the life of the mosquito; we have already discussed the copious intake of blood by the adult female. If we assume that the adult animal assimilates more food than is necessary merely to sustain its own metabolism, then we must search for another energy outlet for stored food reserves. This problem will be

Fig. 1-8. Larva (left) and pupa of *Aedes aegypti*. a, siphon; b, anal papillae; c, food brushes.

analyzed in detail in the following chapter; for the present, it will suffice to say that the entire energy reserve that will sustain the transformation from an aquatic larval form to a terrestrial flying adult is located within the larva. Furthermore, before the adult partakes of its first meal it must have an energy reserve to maintain its flight machinery. Again this reserve was provided for during its ontogeny by a bacterially feeding larva.

Superficially, the problem of growth in the larva appears to be a simple one. The animal feeds continuously; therefore, it is not surprising that it grows continuously. However, recall that the larva is covered externally by a tough, impermeable cuticle. In essence, the tissues of the larva are housed in an indistensible cage, and unless the cage breaks, growth is impossible; if it does break, however, then the tissues of the larva are directly exposed to the surrounding water, and this obviously cannot be.

The mechanism allowing for growth in the larva is an elegant example of how a restriction placed on the animal by an otherwise excellently adapted structure—in this case, the cuticle—is overcome. At precise intervals during its development, the larva molts; that is, it sheds its entire cuticle. This does not mean that it emerges skinless, for beneath the old cuticle a new, highly folded cuticle has already formed. The new cuticle is now free to unfold, and it can even stretch to some extent since for a short time after molting it is somewhat distensible. Unfolding and stretching are made possible because the larva swallows substantial amounts of water. Water intake is actually initiated shortly before the molt, and it plays an important role in enabling the larva to slip out of the old cuticle in the first place. The skin first splits in the head region and then, as the larva drinks and swells, the split proceeds posteriorly and the old cuticle is slipped backward until shed altogether. Once the new cuticle has become properly stretched, it maintains its expanded condition. The excess water is presumably voided from the gut, and the slack in the cuticle is then taken up gradually during the intermolt period as the larva resumes feeding and its tissues grow. Eventually, the animal finds itself strait-jacketed again and it molts once more. There are four larval molts. Molting is the key to growth not only for *Aedes*, but also for all other arthropods, since the possession of a body cuticle is a characteristic of the phylum as a whole.

After the last larval molt, adult development is ready to begin. The transformation of a larval insect to a flying adult is a most mysterious phenomenon, and one that raises intriguing questions. Consider this phenomenon in the following way: as far as biologists are able to determine, the *form* of any particular organism is controlled ultimately by the hereditary units, or genes, passed down to the offspring from the parents (see *Genetics*, in this series). Also, as far as we know, each cell in the body contains the same genes. Therefore, we may say that during larval development the genes preside over the formation of larval tissue. However, the larval form, although it is free living and exists independently from parent tissue, is a transient form and is vastly different from the adult animal. Compare this type of

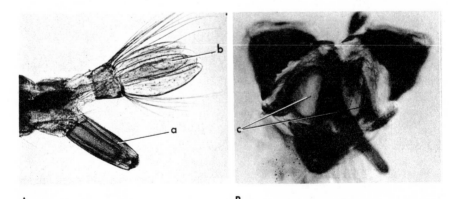

A   **B**

Fig. 1-9. A: Terminal portion of larva, showing siphon, a, and anal papillae, b. B: End view of siphon, showing the two spiracular openings, c, that lead into the tracheal system.

development with that found in humans. We are born as miniature adults and maintain this general form throughout our lifetime. Try to imagine our own situation if we were flying creatures during our early years, then lost our wings, and became wormlike and tunneled underground for our adult life. Do insects such as *Aedes* possess two independent sets of genetic information, one set that presides over adult life, and one that presides over larval life? Or do they possess a single set that presides over both stages of existence, but are the genes somehow modified in their expression during these two periods? These questions remain unanswered at present. It is known, however, that during the larval transformation into the adult animal, entire organ systems are broken down and replaced. Small groups of cells in larval tissue, called *imaginal discs,* ultimately give rise to many of the adult structures (Fig. 1–17). During larval development the imaginal discs are held in abeyance; but after the last larval form, or instar, they develop to completion, at the expense of food reserves laid down by the larva. In this respect they seem almost parasitic as they begin to mold an adult organism within the larval shell.

The change from larva to adult involves some radical transformations. Much of the larval musculature is replaced by adult muscles, and the mouth parts and digestive system undergo major changes. In some insects even the nervous system is almost entirely re-formed. A drastic reorganization of this sort is evidently not compatible with the maintenance of an active existence. During this reorganization, the mosquito abandons the larval stage altogether, and assumes a new form: the pupa. Before its final molt, the larva becomes more plump, especially in the thoracic region, in which the rudiments of adult legs and wings are located (Fig. 1–17). Suddenly the body of the animal gives a pronounced jerk, and comes to lie horizontally just beneath the surface of the water. A major break appears in the cuticle of the thorax, and a pair of respiratory "trumpets" springs out. The cuticle is then displaced backward, and, instead of another larva, the new developmental stage, the pupa, is exposed (Fig. 1–8).

The body of the pupa is composed of a fused head and thorax, or cephalothorax, plus a slender abdomen. The pupa can be considered as a sealed chamber in which an adult organism is forming at the expense of larval tissue. The pupa neither feeds nor eliminates wastes; in fact, its only contact with its environment is through the two respiratory trumpets located on the dorsal surface of the thorax (Fig. 1–11). The pupa is so remarkably insulated from its environment that it can survive for several hours in 70 percent alcohol or even in a 10 percent solution of formaldehyde.

The pupal stage, in spite of the complex development that occurs beneath the cuticle, lasts for only two to three days. This stage is dramatically interrupted when the abdomen suddenly straightens out, and a quick muscular contraction jerks the anterior cephalothorax against the surface film.

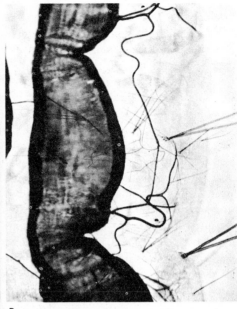

B

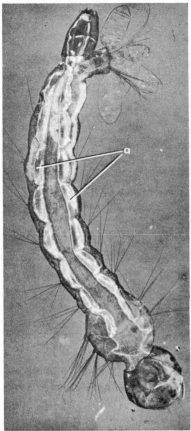

A

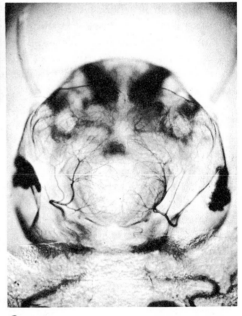

C

Fig. 1-10. A: Larva, showing the two air-filled longitudinal tracheal trunks, a. B: Portion of a tracheal trunk, showing the smaller trachea arising from it. C: Head of larva, with the highly branched tracheae that bring air to the region of the pharyngeal muscles.

A split appears on the cephalothorax, exposing the dry cuticle of the adult. The split widens as the adult swells from the intake of air through its mouth. Then the adult emerges from the pupal case with a steady, smooth motion, giving the impression that it is being pushed out from below (Fig. 1–14). The adult rests on the old pupal cuticle while its wings slowly unfold; within an hour the newly formed *Aedes* is ready to take to the air and initiate the series of events that have been the subject of our discussion thus far.

Although we have devoted several pages to a description of the life cycle of a single species of insect, our discussion so far has been on a rather superficial level. Much remains to be learned about the developmental processes of *Aedes*—as, for that matter, about those of any other organism. Even if all the biologists in the world were to concentrate their energies today upon a study of *Aedes,* we would still not have all the answers in ten or even fifty years. For with each question answered, many new ones would be raised. One might correctly state that to solve the basic problems of the biology of *Aedes* is to solve most of the basic problems of biology itself.

At this point the reader may be struck with the complexity of the development of an animal that he might heretofore have considered to be rather a simple one. It might even seem that *Aedes* has evolved an "unnecessarily" roundabout method of development. Might it not have been just as "sensible" for a mosquito to emerge from the egg as a miniature adult, without going through larval and pupal stages? We, as humans, have a tendency to impose value judgments on all our reasoning. But value judgments may be dangerously misleading when applied to biological thinking. Terms such as "unnecessarily" and "sensible," when used in the above context, are really quite meaningless. The fact is that *Aedes* is eminently successful despite its seemingly roundabout form of development. It is adaptively fit for survival, and *that* is what counts. The fact that the mosquito *has* a larva obviously indicates that this stage is of adaptive significance, and what we should therefore really be asking is, of what particular adaptive value *is* the larval stage of the mosquito? If he ponders this question, the reader may very well conclude that emerging in the form of a miniature adult would really pose for a mosquito some very serious problems of survival. We will have more to say about this later. Biological success is not an easy thing to gauge. It is not even easy to define what we mean by it. It might be said that all species in the world today are successful simply because all are surviving. Yet we know that species do become extinct. The fossil record is laden with ancient forms that exist no more, and we know of species that have become extinct within the recent span of recorded human history. Thus, species that are adaptively successful today may not necessarily be so several hundred or thousand years hence. Perhaps the most notable thing is not so

A

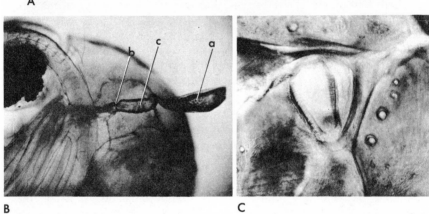

B   C

Fig. 1-11. A: Two young pupae contacting the water surface with their respiratory trumpets. B: Anterior portion of pupa, showing the air-filled respiratory trumpet, a, as it leads inward to the tracheal system. One of the spiracles of the developing adult forms at point b. Later, when the adult emerges, a break occurs at this point so that the respiratory trumpet, plus the portion of trachea, c, that linked it to the adult spiracle, is discarded as part of the pupal cuticle. C: Spiracular opening on the thorax of an adult *Aedes.* There are 16 such spiracles on the thorax and abdomen. Note the fine hairs projecting across the opening and guarding against admission of foreign particles into the tracheal system.

much *which* particular animals and plants are alive today, but that animals and plants *are* alive today, that life still continues to exist three billion years after its inception. Life as a whole, and the process of evolution by which it maintains its changing diversity, has evidently proven its adaptive fitness over a considerable period of time.

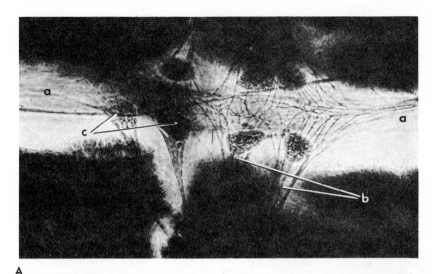

A

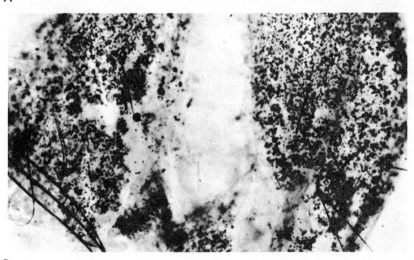

B

Fig. 1-12. A: Portion of the dorsal blood vessel, a, of the *Aedes* larva, showing the alary muscles, b, that effect the dilation of the heart, plus a group of pericardial cells, c. The pericardial cells, judging from their function in other insects, might have an endocrinological function. B: Portion of a segment of a larva stained to show fat. The black spots are fat droplets stored within cells of the fat body.

Thus far, we have outlined several important events and problems faced by *Aedes* during its development. Our intention has been to familiarize the reader with the life cycle of *Aedes* and through the discussion allow the concept of adaptation to crystallize slowly. It is now possible to present a more rigorous analysis of particular problems faced by the animal, and to

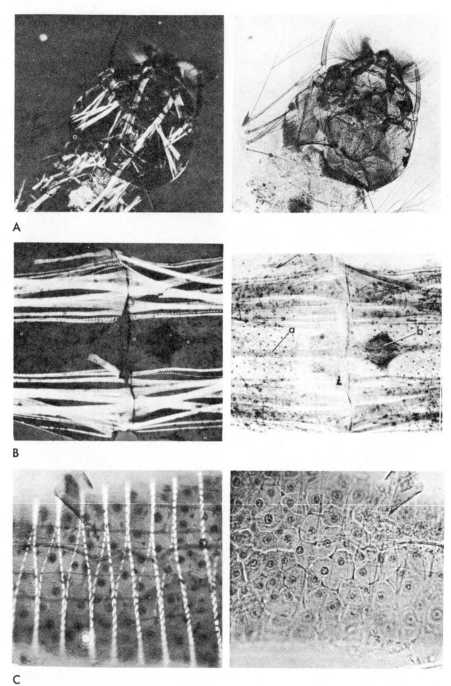

A

B

C

Fig. 1-13.

examine them in their proper perspective through a discussion of how other organisms solve these same problems. Before progressing to this analysis, however, it is worthwhile to note in some detail a few physiological adaptations found in *Aedes*. We have seen, for example, that wings are an excellent adaptation to life in the air, but what of the energy reserves that sustain the wing beat or the muscles that maintain the flight machinery? These factors contribute as much to the general adaptation of flying as the wings themselves. We will continue, then, by discussing physiological aspects of a few organ systems—namely, the respiratory, circulatory, excretory, and osmoregulatory.

RESPIRATORY SYSTEM

Observe any insect in flight and you witness a truly marvelous phenomenon that not only allows the animal to leave the ground, but provides a means through which dispersal of the species, mate location, feeding, and selection of the proper oviposition site are facilitated. When the mechanisms that enable an insect to fly are examined in some detail, it becomes clear that flight is the inevitable outcome of not one, but a great many diverse adaptations.

When we consider, for example, that some insects have wing beats that reach the astounding frequency of several hundred per second, our imagination is staggered. Try tapping your finger as many times as you can on the desk for a period of one minute, employing only finger muscles in the process. You will realize immediately that you are still able to discern strokes and can actually count each beat. You find that toward the end of the minute, your efficiency has greatly lessened and that your finger feels much "weaker" than it did at the start. And with continued tapping, the muscles of your finger begin to hurt and are finally rendered virtually ineffectual. Now imagine the flight muscles in the thorax of an insect (Fig. 1–16) that must contract for minutes on end at a rate that practically parallels in one

Fig. 1-13. (*facing*). Muscles of the larva. Muscles are birefringent, and when examined in polarized light appear conspicuously bright in sharp contrast to the dark non-birefringent structures around them. These photographs are shown in pairs: the ones on the left were taken in polarized light and the ones on the right in ordinary light. A: Head of larva showing the numerous muscles that activate mouth parts, pharynx, and antennae. B: Two consecutive segments of the larval abdomen showing the longitudinal body muscles that stretch from segment to segment. It is by means of these muscles that the larva performs its wiggling motions. The nerve cord, a, and one of the segmental ganglia, b, are seen along the mid-line. C: Surface view of a portion of the mid-gut of the larva (see Fig. 1-6A). The very fine and neatly arranged circular muscles that spiral around the gut effect peristalsis.

second our rate for one minute. Insect flight muscles may contract up to 50 times per second and continue at this rate for extended periods of time. Why doesn't the insect fall to the ground in fatigue after a minute of flight? How can a honeybee, for example, fly over a distance of several miles to its hive and then, after depositing pollen in the hive, fly off again at the same speed to the same distant pollen source?

Part of the answer emerges from a study of the animal's respiratory system. When we run fast, we experience an oxygen lack and begin to breathe hard. In order for muscular activity to be sustained, an adequate supply of oxygen must be available to the muscle cells, and carbon dioxide must be rapidly removed as it accumulates in the cells. Often after running we find that although we are breathing in large quantities of air, our muscles continue to feel cramped and painful. This is because our breathing rate is not the only factor that determines how much oxygen is reaching our muscle cells; rather, the limiting factor is the circulatory system, which carries the oxygen from lungs to muscles.

Here is where the insect is at an advantage over man. Cells in insects breathe in a different way from our own. Virtually each cell is directly connected to the atmosphere by breathing tubes, or *tracheae*. To use a rather homely description, we may say that each cell breathes through a hollow straw that opens directly to the atmosphere. Since insects are small, no insect cell is ever far removed from a rich oxygen supply. In humans, oxygen must pass through the lung membrane, through a capillary wall, and into the blood stream, where it becomes associated with a red blood cell. The rate of diffusion of oxygen through water is 1,000,000 times slower than it is through air. Thus, the advantages of an air-filled tracheal system are obvious: the only barrier that separates the insect flight muscle cell from atmospheric oxygen is the cell membrane.

In the developing embryo the tracheal system is formed by an ingrowth, or invagination, of epidermal cells. Once the epidermal cells invaginate, they secrete a lining, or cuticle, that appears to be identical with one of the layers of cuticle that covers the exterior of the animal. As the invaginated tubes, or tracheae, penetrate the tissues of the animal they branch into smaller and smaller tubules (Fig. 1–10), in much the same manner that larger blood vessels in vertebrates branch into smaller vessels and finally capillaries. The tiny terminal tracheae, called tracheoles, actually penetrate individual cells, pushing the cell membranes inward as they penetrate, or they may come to lie in close contact with cells without actually penetrating them.

We have stated that the tracheal system is air filled. What keeps the tracheae from filling with tissue fluids, and what prevents their collapse in an animal that is continually distorting its body through locomotory and

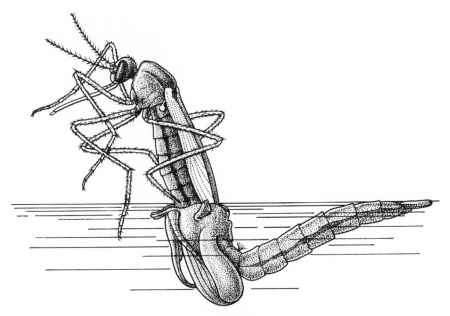

Fig. 1-14. Adult mosquito emerging from its pupal shell. (After R. E. Snodgrass.)

other movements? The answer to the first question is simple: the thin cuticle that lines the tracheal system is, like its thicker counterpart of the body wall, impermeable to water. The single property of cuticle impermeability has two-fold adaptive significance in insects. In the body wall it prevents water loss to the surrounding atmosphere; in the trachea it prevents flooding of the respiratory passages and impairment of the efficiency of the breathing mechanism.

The tracheae are also adapted in a special way that enables them to withstand outside pressure changes without collapsing. During development, the cuticle of the tracheal system is laid down in a spiral or helical fashion, in the manner of a spring. The result of this unusual architecture is that although the trachea is, like a spring, capable of considerable longitudinal extension, it is virtually incapable of being compressed laterally. Thus, muscular contractions, and other distorting influences, do not cause obliteration of the tracheal lumen. On the other hand, since the tracheae are capable of longitudinal extension, any organ to which they attach is capable of considerable movement or shifting without breaking contact with its oxygen supply.

Since, as we reasoned earlier, an insect in flight has a truly formidable oxygen demand, and since the tracheal system is an efficient respiratory system admirably adapted to fulfill this demand, it might be tempting to con-

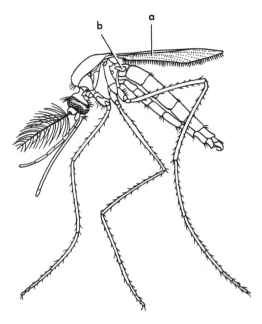

Fig. 1-15. Aedes aegypti (male) showing the wing, a, and haltere, b, of the left side. Most insects have two pairs of wings, but in mosquitoes and other members of the order Diptera, the second pair of wings has become reduced to form the short knobby halteres. The halteres act as gyroscopes, indispensable for the control of flight (see also Fig. 1-16). (After R. E. Snodgrass.)

clude that a tracheal system represents a specific adaptation to flight. However, tracheal systems have evolved several times independently among arthropods, and many of these do not fly at all. Certain spiders, ticks, silverfish, and whip scorpions all possess tracheae, but none of them have wings. There is even a tracheal system in a nonarthropod—specifically, a many-legged wormlike animal called *Peripatus* (Fig. 3–18), which lives in damp vegetation under decaying logs and which some biologists believe to be closely related to the direct ancestors of arthropods.

The conclusion must be that although the tracheal system was probably a preadaptation that greatly facilitated the subsequent evolution of flight in insects, it did not evolve concurrently or subsequently to the acquisition of wings. If we speculate on the evolution of the tracheal system, we should look at the various tracheated forms and attempt to discover a common denominator that can account for its existence in *all* of them. Such a search reveals one salient point: although not all animals with tracheal systems are flying forms, all tracheated forms possess an external cuticle. It appears that once a terrestrial form evolved an appropriately impermeable cuticle, then the development of an internal system of cuticular respiratory tubes was almost a necessary consequence. Many of. the forms that evolved this system remained relatively sluggish in their locomotory activities, but this sluggishness is not attributable to deficiencies in their respiratory apparatus. The possession of a tracheal system betowed upon its bearers an evolutionary potential for vastly improving their locomotory capabilities. The flying insect, whose muscular energy output probably has no parallel among other tracheated arthropods, represents the crowning achievement in the realization of this potential.

CIRCULATORY SYSTEM

The circulatory system of an insect is remarkably simple when compared to, for instance, our own. In man, as in all vertebrates, the blood has, among other functions, the very important one of distributing dissolved respiratory gases. An adequate distribution of these gases is made possible by the possession of a complex system of arteries, veins, and capillaries, through which the blood courses rapidly and in a fixed traffic pattern between the various tissues and the lungs or gills. In an insect, the respiratory system is in no way linked to or dependent upon the circulatory system for its proper operation. It is therefore not surprising that an insect has neither an elaborate vessel system nor a strongly muscled heart such as is needed to pump blood through narrow tubes.

The so-called heart of an insect consists of a thin-walled, dorsal tube, perforated by valvular openings, or *ostia,* and extending along the entire length of the abdomen and thorax, eventually opening anteriorly into the head cavity. It is attached to the body wall by a series of fan-shaped muscles, called alary muscles (Fig. 1–12). When the heart contracts, its circumference is decreased and blood is forced out into the head region. Once outside the heart, the blood does not follow fixed pathways along arteries or veins but forms an internal pool, filling up all of the spaces between the organs. In other words, rather than being irrigated by capillaries, the organs of the insect are, as it were, suspended in blood and bathed by it. A body cavity that is blood-filled is called a hemocoele.

The blood in the hemocoele is not stagnant. When the heart relaxes after its contraction, it is expanded to its original condition under the action of the alary muscles; the ostia open, and blood is sucked in from the area around the heart. The next contraction forces blood out anteriorly again into the hemocoele. In addition to the stirring of blood caused by heart contraction, blood is continually being sloshed around by the muscular movements during locomotion and by movements of the gut. The faster an insect runs or flies, the more its blood is mixed about in the hemocoele. This becomes very important during flight because, although the blood does not carry oxygen to the flight muscles, it does carry food materials to fuel their contractions. Thus, the activities of the very muscles whose metabolic demands are increasing improve the circulation that helps meet these demands. Actually, in an insect, stored food never has far to travel in order to reach an organ that needs it. In *Aedes,* as in insects generally, food reserves, including large amounts of stored fats, are distributed throughout the animal in a tissue called the fat body (Fig. 1–12). This tissue, in the form of more or less irregular clusters of cells, can be found virtually anywhere in the spaces between the various organs.

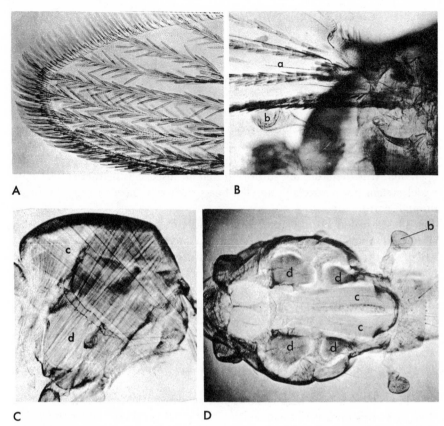

Fig. 1-16. A: Tip of wing of *Aedes,* beset with scales. The adaptive significance of the scales remains to be demonstrated. B: Portion of base of right wing, a, with haltere, b, immediately behind it (see also halteres, b, in D). C and D: Sagittal (C) and frontal (D) sections of thorax showing the powerful longitudinal, c, and dorsoventral, d, flight muscles.

REGULATION OF INTERNAL ENVIRONMENT

A remarkable feature of the living state is that despite continual fluctuations in the environment, the internal milieu of the organism is strikingly constant. The maintenance of this constancy will be the final subject of discussion in this chapter. We shall begin by examining a few basic problems faced by *Aedes* and analyze them in terms of homeostatic mechanisms.

One of the greatest problems facing any terrestrial creature is that of water loss. Before any chemical reaction can occur in a living system, water must be present; in the complete absence of water, living cells perish. Organisms on land, regardless of their protective mechanisms, are always slowly desiccating, and if water is not brought back into the system, the organism eventually dies. Thus, terrestrial creatures, although they are not totally able to prevent water loss, have devised mechanisms that minimize this loss and others that provide for water intake. If the water level of an animal remains relatively constant throughout its life, we know that some homeostatic mechanism must be operating. As we proceed with the discussion, consider an adult *Aedes* living in an area where the daily temperatures may rise to 120° F, and try to imagine methods the animal might employ to guard against desiccation.

Another problem faced by all living organisms is that of eliminating undesirable products of metabolism. Among the end products of protein metabolism in all animals are nitrogen-containing compounds. A common end product of this type is ammonia. Ammonia is a highly toxic substance, and if it is not eliminated from living systems as fast as it is formed, death results. We shall see that aquatic organisms lose their ammonia by simply dissolving it in excess water and then passing this water into the surrounding medium. But what of the terrestrial animal, which must continually guard against water loss? Can it afford continually to pass out ammonia-laden water from its system? How might the adult *Aedes* be able to eliminate nitrogenous wastes and still maintain a fairly constant water level within its tissues?

Finally, there is the problem of salt balance in organisms. Several of the elements—for example, sodium, potassium, chlorine, magnesium, and sulfur—that are requisite for life enter the body in the form of salts dissolved in water. Pure sodium is lethal, but in the form of sodium chloride, or table salt, it is not only nontoxic, but essential. One of the functions of salts is to provide for the proper osmotic environment inside and around the cells of a living system. We know that if we eat an excess of salt, we become thirsty. Excess salt in the system causes water to leave the cells through osmosis and to collect in extracellular spaces. This results in swelling, or edema. Thus, we drink large quantities of water to make up for the water loss from our cells. Organisms, as a rule, cannot withstand wide fluctuations in their salt content, and many of them possess highly effective salt-regulating mechanisms with which to counteract any tendency toward departure from the normal osmotic balance. The feeling of thirst after a salty meal is in a sense illustrative of man's own salt-regulating mechanism. But *Aedes* may also have its share of osmotic problems. Think of a larva in a tree hole, suddenly exposed to a one-inch rainfall. If the tree hole is small, this might well result in a doubling of the water in it. Rainwater is relatively salt-free, and the salt concentration in the water would be reduced to half. Can the larva maintain a constant internal salt concentration despite this sudden dilution of the medium around it?

We have now focused on three of the many problems that an animal must face if it is to maintain the constant internal environment necessary

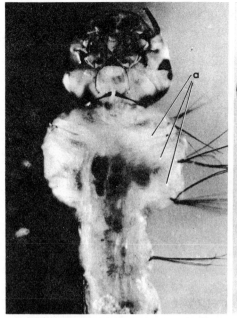

A

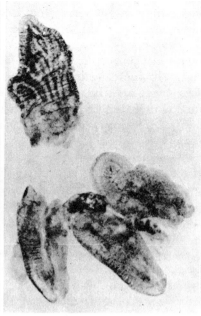

B

C

Fig. 1-17. A: Ventral view of anterior end of mature larva. The imaginal discs of the adult legs, a, can already be seen inside the thorax. B: Imaginal discs of the adult legs and wing of one side, dissected from a larva of comparable developmental age as the one in (A). C: Profile view of head of larva showing the functional larval eye, a, and the nonfunctional developing eye of the adult, b.

for life: water preservation, excretion of nitrogenous waters, and salt regulation. Let us now examine how these problems may be solved.

A single adaptation that plays an important role in minimizing water loss in terrestrial insects has already been mentioned, namely, the possession of an impermeable external cuticle. Outermost on the cuticle of insects is a very thin layer of wax only a few microns thick. This waxy layer prevents not only the passage of water from the tissues outward, but also the entrance into the body of water from the outside. In the adult mosquito, the possession of an impermeable body is of critical importance for survival in air. But some water is invariably lost through the tracheal system. Where the terminal tracheal branches end in cells, the tracheal walls are water permeable. This is necessary in order for there to be a proper exchange of respiratory gases at this level. As a result, some water invariably evaporates into the lumen of the trachea and eventually this water is unavoidably lost through the outer openings (spiracles) of the tracheal system (Fig. 1–11). In the larval *Aedes* there are only two such openings, situated, as will be recalled, at the end of the siphon, and the loss of water is therefore not very substantial. It is, at any rate, of no great consequence, since the larva has access to ample water and can readily replenish whatever is lost. But in the adult mosquito there is a total of 16 spiracles, situated in rows on both sides of the thorax and abdomen. Were it not for the fact that the spiracles of most insects are endowed with valves that are opened only when the respiratory demands of the animal so dictate, the water loss from the tracheal system would be considerably greater than it actually is.

Although the foregoing might imply that terrestrial insects must at one time or other drink water in order to make up for losses such as occur through the tracheal system, the fact is that some insects do not drink at all. The common end products of carbohydrate and fat metabolism are carbon dioxide and water. During extensive fat utilization, large quantities of water are liberated into the system—much more than through carbohydrate metabo-

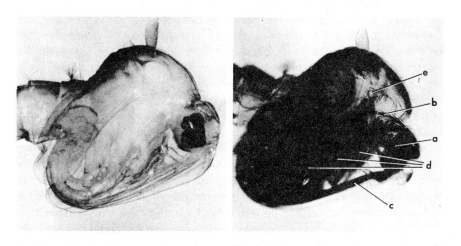

A   B

Fig. 1-18. Front end of a young pupa (A), and of a mature one (B). Notice how in the latter some of the adult structures are already recognizable: head, a; antenna, b; beak, c; legs, d; spiracle, e. The same spiracle is shown enlarged in Fig. 1-11C.

lism. This water, known as metabolic water, is no different from the water in a pond and is equally useful for the sustenance of life. Therefore, the act of flying, or even walking, may produce a significant share of metabolic water. An animal such as a clothesmoth, for example, never takes a drink during its entire larval life, relying completely on fat reserves for its water supply.

As we stated earlier, the elimination of nitrogenous wastes may impose a dangerous stress upon an animal's water economy. An animal loses water during urination because nitrogenous end products of protein metabolism are usually toxic and must be dissolved in water before their elimination from the system. In insects, the nitrogenous end product of protein metabolism is uric acid. Uric acid is a much larger molecule than ammonia, is relatively nontoxic, and only slightly soluble in water. The excretory organs of an insect are large and slender tubes called Malpighian tubules (Fig. 1–6), which are closed at one end and open by the other into the last portion of the intestine. Uric acid is secreted into the tubules in aqueous solution, and gradually, as the urine passes down each tubule toward the intestine, water is withdrawn and reabsorbed into the blood. The net result is that uric acid is passed to the outside in crystalline form with the feces, with hardly any water loss at all. Thus, an insect can afford to maintain a high level of protein metabolism without having to sacrifice a large amount of water to eliminate the resulting nitrogenous wastes.

The ability to produce uric acid has some other important consequences for an insect. Both the egg and pupa are developmental stages in which the animal is virtually sealed off from the environment. Except for the respiratory gas exchange, nothing enters or leaves the animal. Yet these stages are by no means metabolically dormant. As the embryo develops inside the egg, or the adult is shaped from larval tissues inside the pupa, the metabolic machinery is operating in high gear. New proteins are being formed, and some are being degraded; with this degradation there occurs the inevitable production of nitrogenous wastes. Since neither the egg nor the pupa can drink, they cannot afford to produce a nitrogenous waste such as ammonia, which must be washed from the system in dilute aqueous urine. The fact that the end product is uric acid relieves the egg and pupa from the need of eliminating their nitrogenous wastes. Uric acid can be stored inside their bodies as harmless crystals until such time as the emerging larva or adult is free to pass the crystals to the outside. Many insects when they emerge from the pupa will at once defecate, and among these wastes can be found large quantities of uric acid crystals.

The larva of *Aedes*, having ample access to fresh water, does not face the same problem as the terrestrial adult regarding the elimination of nitrogenous wastes. It also produces uric acid, but this is sometimes eliminated in solution with copious amounts of water.

For the adult mosquito, water conservation is obviously of paramount

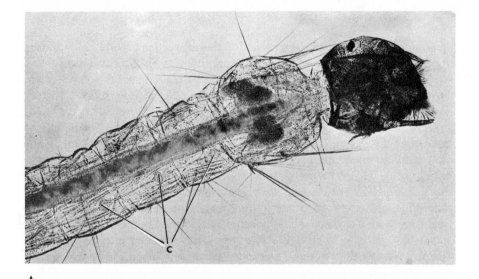

A

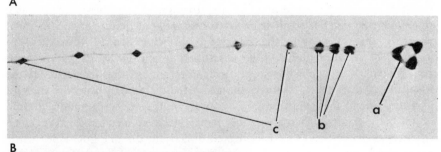

B

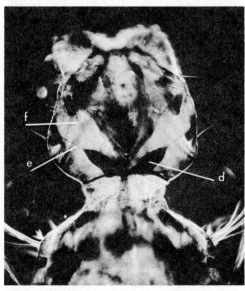

C

Fig. 1-19. A: Larva rendered translucent by immersion in glycerine. The digestive tract is visible (compare with Fig. 1-6), as well as a portion of the ventral nerve cord (c, ganglia). B: Isolated nerve cord of mosquito larva: a, brain; b, thoracic ganglia; c, abdominal ganglia. C: Head of larva, specially illuminated to show the brain, d, with the optic nerve, e, and antennal nerve, f.

importance, and we have seen some of the adaptations that help minimize the loss of water. Oddly enough, there are times when the adult must guard against introducing too much water into its system. An excess of water can be as harmful as a lack of it, since in either case the delicate osmotic balance necessary for survival is upset. Both the adult male and female occasionally drink aqueous fluids. If the water were absorbed into their bodies all at once, then the resulting osmotic dilution of the blood would prove fatal. There is a neat adaptive mechanism that prevents this all-out absorption from taking place. The anterior part of the digestive system, the foregut (Fig. 1-6), is lined by cuticle similar to that which covers the body surface. No absorption of water can occur in this region. Attached to the foregut are one large and two small blind pouches, or diverticuli, similarly lined with impervious cuticle. Behind the fore-gut is the so-called mid-gut, which is the seat of most digestive and absorptive processes. When the animal drinks, the water is not passed directly into the mid-gut for absorption, but is first shunted off into the diverticuli of the fore-gut. From these impermeable reservoirs the water is then delivered to the mid-gut gradually and in small amounts, thus preventing the mid-gut from being flooded with excessive amounts of a dilute fluid whose absorption it apparently cannot prevent. Experimentally it is possible to put a ligature around the diverticuli. If the mosquito is then given a drink, the liquid passes directly into the mid-gut and the animal dies, apparently as a result of the sudden osmotic dilution of its body fluids. When the adult female takes a blood meal, the blood bypasses the diverticuli and is delivered directly to the mid-gut. Since vertebrate blood is of an osmotic concentration not much different from that of the mosquito's own blood, its admission into the mid-gut can be tolerated. Nothing is known about the sensory mechanisms by which the animal gauges the osmotic qualities of the meal that determine its subsequent delivery into one or the other compartment of the gut.

The problem faced by an adult *Aedes* when it drinks water is one that, in a sense, is faced by the larva at all times. The larva is, after all, surrounded by water that is usually of an osmotic concentration below that of its own body fluids, and this water, unless prevented from doing so, would diffuse through the body wall of the animal and flood its insides. Here again the waxy covering of the cuticle comes into play. In the adult, this layer serves primarily to prevent water loss; in the larva it prevents the influx of water from the outside. It will also be recalled that the larva minimizes the amount of water taken into the gut through feeding by straining out useful solids and regurgitating the water before it is actually swallowed.

The problem of salt regulation is one with which we shall only briefly deal here; considerable attention will be devoted to the subject in the next chapter. Although most of the body surface of the larval *Aedes* is water impermeable, there is one area that is permeable. This is the surface of the anal papillae (Fig. 1-9), which extend prominently from the last abdominal segment. Through these papillae water and salts may be absorbed from the surrounding water. If the body fluids in the animal are hypotonic to the surrounding water (can you think of natural circumstances in which this is likely to apply for an *Aedes* larva?), water and salts pass into the hemocoele and are excreted via the Malpighian tubules. However, as they pass through the last portion of the gut (rectum, Fig. 1-6), the salts are reabsorbed. The net result of this absorption is the conservation of salt and the production of a hypotonic urine. When the salt content of the internal medium increases, the salt content of the urine in the excretory tubules is also increased. However, salt absorption in the rectum decreases, resulting in the elimination of salts. The precise mechanisms that determine when salts will be absorbed and when they will be excreted are not known. Nevertheless, we know that through the regulation imposed by the anal papillae, the Malpighian tubules, and the rectum, the salt content of the internal milieu is kept relatively constant. In the adult animal the excretory organs and rectum may possibly also serve to control the amounts of salts voided or withheld, but very little precise information is available on how these mechanisms operate.

The problems of water conservation, excretion of nitrogenous wastes, and salt regulation are closely related. The type of nitrogenous end product produced by an animal will influence the amount of water lost as urine; the level of various salts in the tissues ultimately determines how much water will be withdrawn from or enter the cells of the animal. Suffice it to say for the present that *Aedes* possesses a diversity of structural and physiological adaptations operating to meet the need for maintaining a constant internal milieu. No single adaptation answers all of the problems, or even one of the problems, concerned with osmoregulation.

We began by confronting the reader with an animal and stating that by living with this animal for some time he would be better equipped to appreciate a concept of adaptation than if he were simply given a concrete definition. We have attempted to demonstrate adaptation on several different levels—the behavioral, the structural, the physiological, and even the molecular. If a concept of adaptation is not beginning to crystallize in his mind by this time, the reader will have at least recognized that the life of the mosquito is beset with problems. Further, it should be obvious that for every major problem that exists, the animal possesses a mechanism or group of mechanisms operating to meet it. It is because these mechanisms are operating to the obvious advantage of the animal that we say, "This animal is adapted for survival in the world of today." Our very definition of life or "aliveness" supposes adaptation. After the publication of Darwin's great treatise on evolution, Spencer coined the phrase "survival of the fittest." The fit animal is the one that survives and the animal that survives is the one that is fit. We can substitute the term "adapted" for "fit" and the aphorism still holds. If we devote pages to pinpointing particular mechanisms that contribute to an animal's survival, and end by saying, "For these reasons the animal is adapted," the reader may well answer, "Of course, the animal is adapted. If it weren't, then it wouldn't be around for us to study."

But there is a good deal more to the concept of adaptation. So far we have looked at one animal, *Aedes aegypti,* and we have looked at it through a long and narrow tube. We have considered it as a single isolated living entity, and we have given no thought to the multitude of other animals with which it shares the world. Let us now change our approach and examine *Aedes* in a broader perspective. Let us compare the animal to others. As soon as we do this we shall become aware of an important fact: the problems faced by *Aedes* in its struggle for survival are really not at all unique. Other animals face similar ones. But the ways that different animals are adapted to solve similar problems are not necessarily the same. The world of living animals is not to be viewed as an assemblage that meets the life challenge with certain pat mechanisms common to all. The challenge may be the same, but the ways of meeting it are as diverse as the world of life itself. In short, the road to biological success is not necessarily the straight and narrow one.

The questions we shall ask in the next chapter are not profound ones. Why do most fresh-water animals lack free-living larval forms? Why is the egg of a terrestrial animal usually larger than that of an aquatic one? Why are there so few insects in the ocean? What are the adaptive advantages to feeding discontinuously rather than continuously? These questions are not *meant* to be profound ones. Neither were the ones we have been asking so far about *Aedes.* The nature of the questions is really irrelevant. What concerns us is the type of approach to finding the answers. And in the next chapter our approach will be different from what it was in the first. We shall look at adaptation in a comparative context.

SUGGESTED READING LIST

CHRISTOPHERS, S. R., 1960. *Aedes aegypti* (*L.*). New York: Cambridge University Press.

ROEDER, K. D., 1953. *Insect physiology.* New York: Wiley.

ROTH, L. M., "A study of mosquito behavior. An experimental laboratory study of the sexual behavior of *Aedes aegypti* (Linnaeus)," *The American Midland Naturalist,* Vol. 40 (1948), pp. 265–352.

WIGGLESWORTH, V. B., 1953. *The principles of insect physiology.* London: Methuen.

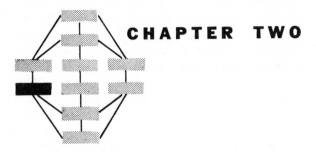

CHAPTER TWO

A

CASE STUDY

IN PERSPECTIVE We can conveniently begin our

analysis of adaptive mechanisms in the mosquito by focusing on the three main topics that formed the basis of our narrative in the first chapter. The first topic, which emphasizes behavioral adaptations, is *reproduction,* and under this category we will consider phenomena such as mate location and oviposition. Second, we will discuss *development* and analyze in perspective the adaptive significance of the different developmental stages in *Aedes'* existence. Finally, we will discuss the general problem of *maintenance of the internal environment* and compare various physiological adaptations of *Aedes* to those of other forms of life.

REPRODUCTION

Reproduction is a general attribute of life. The very definition of organism implies the capacity to reproduce. One usually associates reproduction with sexuality, and it is therefore not at all surprising that there are two kinds of adult *Aedes,* males and females, which through courtship and mating contribute jointly to the propagation of the species. But reproduction is not always associated with sex. There are many organisms that reproduce both sexually and asexually (sometimes having a regular alternation of sexual and asexual generations) and there are others that reproduce only asexually (for example, *Amoeba*). Sexuality, then, is widespread but not universal. What are the relative adaptive merits of sexual and asexual reproduction?

Sexual vs. Asexual Reproduction

The essential feature of sexual reproduction is fertilization: the fusion of sperm and egg to form a zygote. The new individual that develops from this zygote is endowed with a genetic complement that stems from both parents, rather than from either of them alone. The net result is that off-spring produced by sexual reproduction tend to be unlike either parent, since they incorporate genes from both of them in new combinations. Sexual reproduction is thus viewed as a mechanism that promotes variability among the individuals of a species; with each new generation, new genetic formulas are introduced into the population. This is extremely important from an evolutionary standpoint, since one of the major safeguards that a species has against extinction is the variability of its individuals. If all individuals were exactly alike—that is, genetically identical—then there would be no differential susceptibility among the individuals of the species to the pressures of natural selection operating upon them. Natural selection would affect all individuals in the same way, and should the environment become incom-patible to survival, this incompatibility would not affect just a few individuals but would threaten and could eventually doom the species as a whole. Diver-sity is essential if a species is to retain the potential for evolution. (Actually, there are other more subtle aspects to the significance of sexual reproduction; see *Evolution* and *Genetics,* in this series.)

In asexual reproduction, the offspring are genetically identical to the parents. Cell division in *Amoeba,* for instance, as far as we know always results in the production of identical genetic twins. This does not mean, of course, that all individuals of a species of *Amoeba* are identical, and that the species will perpetuate itself without change indefinitely. Mutations occur in the genes of *Amoeba* as in those of other species of organisms. But when-ever a mutation appears in *Amoeba,* it is bound to remain associated with the particular genetic formula of the individual in which it first occurred. In the absence of sexual reproduction there is no way for this mutant gene to be distributed through the population and eventually incorporated into new genetic formulas prevailing in other individuals of the species. This can be a handicap, since a particular mutation need not necessarily be at its adaptive best within the particular genetic formula of the original bearer. It might be of selective advantage only to an individual of entirely different genetic constitution. By limiting the possibility for genetic recombinations, asexual reproduction imposes a very definite restriction upon the evolutionary potential of a species. There is therefore obvious adaptive significance to sex, and its widespread occurrence should come as no surprise. But it is also significant that some organisms, such as *Amoeba,* reproduce only asexually. Admittedly these are the exception, but as is always the case with exceptions to biological rules, the very fact that they do occur should give pause for thought. *Amoeba* is particularly interesting because it seems possible that asexual reproduction was only secondarily adopted by these Protozoa. Their ancestors might well have reproduced sexually. One is therefore led to inquire about the particular circumstances under which is it likely to be adaptively advantageous for a species to forego sexual reproduction in favor of asexual reproduction. In other words, under what conditions might it be of selective advantage to reduce rather than to enhance the potential for variability? We leave these questions for the reader to ponder.

Sex is not restricted to higher organisms. The complicated process of conjugation, shown by *Paramecium* (Fig. 2–1) and other ciliated

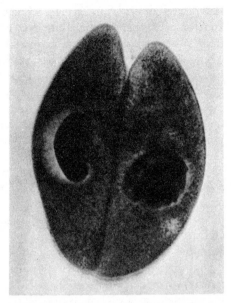

Fig. 2-1. Two *Paramecium* in conjugation.

Protozoa, and which involves the reciprocal transfer of micronuclei between temporarily paired individuals, is essentially a sexual process, since the two conjugants, as a result of the exchange of genetic material between them, emerge with new genetic formulas. Even certain bacteria are known to have mechanisms for exchanging genetic material between one another.

Mate Location

Gametes are single cells, and as a rule are relatively short lived. Moreover, they can survive only in an aqueous medium, and they require such a medium for fertilization. In organisms that reproduce sexually we can therefore expect to find mechanisms that bring the sexes within close proximity of one another in anticipation of the release and fertilization of their gametes. On land there is the special problem of the desiccating effect of the environment, which requires that an aqueous medium compatible with fertilization be provided by the parents or otherwise made available. We have seen how *Aedes* finds its mate, and how through copulation it ensures that fertilization occurs in the moisture-laden genital tract of the female. Other organisms face the same problems, but there is enormous diversity in the particular solutions they have evolved to meet them.

Aedes is an animal that can move about. Hence the male *can* fly to the female. But how is fertilization accomplished in organisms that do not lead a free life? Many species of clams, barnacles, colonial coelenterates, and tunicates spend their adult lives in dense crowds. For them the critical thing is to release their gametes more or less simultaneously; their proximity guarantees fertilization. Also, fertilization need not be internal as in *Aedes,* since the gametes can survive in the water in which the animals live. *Venus,* the common quahog, for instance, lives in "clam beds" where the individuals are in close association with their neighbors. When the animals are sexually mature they retain their gametes within their bodies until they receive the proper stimulus for their expulsion. In this case the proper stimulation is the emission of gametes by another individual in the form of a white cloud of seminal fluid. This fluid, when drawn in through the siphon of an adjacent clam, stimulates the animal to emit its gametes. The senior author has observed a tank of about four dozen clams, in which one animal emitted its gametes. Within a matter of seconds other individuals began to discharge, and within minutes the 15-gallon aquarium was so concentrated with seminal fluid that the water was virtually opaque.

It is logical to ask what initiates the emission of gametes in the first individual that discharges. The answer is not known. Possibly each animal, upon reaching sexual maturity, emits a few of its gametes, retaining the remainder until it receives from the surrounding sea water a stimulus that signals that others nearby are responding similarly. Although the chemical factors responsible for inducing gametic discharge remain unknown, it should be obvious that the possession on the part of a crowded sessile organism of a mechanism that ensures collective and synchronous gamete emission is of adaptive value.

Temporary crowding at the time of mating is not uncommon in free-living organisms. The clamworm *Neanthes* (a polychaete annelid) swims to the surface of the ocean during mating time. In areas where *Neanthes* abounds, hundreds and hundreds of animals collect in the surface layers of water and then spawn. Available evidence indicates that spawning time is determined by particular phases of the moon, and that the stimulus attracting the animals to the surface of the water is solely light.

Probably one of the most striking mechanisms that assures that sexually mature animals are in the same place at the same time is that of another polychaete, the palolo worm, *Leodice.* This animal inhabits the reefs of the Southern Pacific. When the last quarter of the October-November moon dawns, the posterior half of the body of the worm is constricted off. These posterior fragments then rise to the surface in tremendous numbers. Spawning occurs and fertilization is immediate. The anterior end begins to regenerate the posterior fragment, and a whole year passes before another spawning occurs. In this remarkable case, only the reproductive portion of the animal collects in a particular environment to ensure the crowded conditions necessary for fertilization.

There are a great many animals, such as *Aedes,* in which males and females are brought together simply in pairs, rather than in whole mating aggregations. The particular circumstances under which pairing is brought about vary greatly. In aquatic animals, pairing does not necessarily lead to copulation and internal fertilization. The male and female may merely discharge their gametes once they are in close proximity, and fertilization takes place in the water around them. This occurs in many fish and amphibians. But on land, where gametes cannot survive exposure, copulation is the rule. Internal fertilization, such as occurs in *Aedes,* is characteristic of all major groups of terrestrial animals, including insects, reptiles, birds, and mammals. The particular mechanisms that bring the sexes together are extraordinarily diverse. In *Aedes,* sound is involved: the flying female emits what is essentially a mating call. Mating calls are produced by forms as different as moose, crickets, and spring peepers. But sound is just one way in which pairing may be mediated. Sometimes chemical or visual stimuli are involved, or—perhaps most commonly—a combination of stimuli of different kinds. The insects themselves offer a wide range of examples of sex attractant mechanisms.

Fire flies, for instance, lure one another by light flashes. A given species may have a flash pattern all its own. Thus in areas where several species coexist, the uniqueness of the "language" of each prevents improper pairing from taking place as a result of mistaken identity.

In a species of cockroach (*Periplaneta americana;* Fig. 2–7) the female releases a chemical secretion that "alerts" males to her presence nearby. Less than 100 molecules of secretion can excite a male. The existence of this chemical can easily be demonstrated by a simple experiment. A group of females (preferably virgin or nonpregnant females, which seem to be the richest sources of secretion) are confined for a few days in a jar lined with absorbent filter paper. When this paper is subsequently transferred to another jar with males, these will begin scurrying about with their wings fluttering, showing a behavior that is unmistakably that of courting cockroaches. The paper, laden with secretion, is evidently mistaken for the female. Mosquitoes, you will recall, can also be misled, when their "mating call" is mimicked with a tuning fork.

Chemical sex attractants are produced by certain moths. The female is the source of attractant, and she can advertise her presence for great distances around her. It used to be thought that the male homes in on the female by flying along the gradient of increasing molecular concentration of attractant. However, it can be shown mathematically that the attractant is distributed virtually uniformly after it has diffused a few feet away from the female, and that there is therefore no long-range gradient for the male to follow. What actually happens is that the male, when he first scents the attractant, takes to flight and proceeds upwind, therefore inevitably moving toward the female. Once at close range, he is then guided to his mark by following the concentration gradient.

Many insects have good vision, and in diurnal forms sex recognition may sometimes be primarily on the basis of sight. This is probably true for many butterflies and wasps. Remarkably little research has been done on this topic. It would be interesting to know whether a given sex can be attracted simply by "showing" it an artificial model of the other. Nature has provided us with a remarkable parallel to this experiment. There are certain orchids, the flowers of which mimic female wasps. The males are attracted to the female images on the flowers, mount them, and even attempt to copulate with them. In the process they pick up pollen, which is then conveyed to the next flower they mount. For the orchid, this peculiar association is a means of promoting cross-pollination. But it also demonstrates that vision plays a major role in the courtship of these wasps. In fact, if one were to analyze carefully the female features that are reproduced on the flower, one could neatly resolve the particular image characteristics that the male normally relies upon for recognizing the female.

Thus, by employing either sight, hearing, smell, or a combination of senses, animals "solve" the problem of mate location in diverse ways. The evolution that led to the mating pattern as we know it in *Aedes* today involved the adaptive refinement of a variety of anatomical and physiological systems. If we studied critically the same pattern in any other animal, we would ultimately see that mating involves no less complicated an interaction between a diversity of adaptive mechanisms.

We should now be asking ourselves numerous questions. Earlier, when we focused on reproduction and viewed it as a universal characteristic of life, we inquired about the relative adaptive merits of the two major alternatives, sexual and asexual reproduction, by which this characteristic finds expression. In dealing now with a more special problem, mate location, we are again faced with the fact that alternative solutions—this time, a great many of them—have evolved to meet a single adaptive requirement. We could therefore again proceed with a line of inquiry designed to analyze the special adaptive merits of each alternative solution. Rather than doing so, we shall merely present the reader with a sample of the type of questions one could pose in undertaking such an analysis. Some of these questions we shall turn to later in a different context, but most of them are left for the reader to pursue. What might be the special environmental circumstances that would favor the evolution of a sex attractant mechanism such as that of the mosquito—that is, a sound-mediated mechanism—and how do these circumstances differ from those that would favor the evolution of attractant mechanisms based on chemical or visual stimuli? Would one expect aquatic animals such as fish to attract one another by chemical stimuli, or would one expect sound or visual cues to predominate? What common characteristics do organisms have that live in dense colonies or that form temporary aggregations at mating time, and what differentiates these organisms from those that mate in pairs? Organisms that mate in pairs often must spend a good deal of their adult time searching for a mate. In what special way must these organisms be adapted in order to devote so much time in pursuit of a single goal?

Questions such as these are part of the very essence of biological thinking. They lead to the types of abstractions and generalizations without which the living world around us would remain the bewildering array of diversity that it so obviously is at first glance.

Oviposition

Once a female *Aedes* has mated, she actively seeks out the proper site in which to lay her eggs. Again, as in the finding of a mate, we are dealing here with a specialized behavior which if analyzed in detail could be resolved into a series of stimulus-and-response mechanisms that guide the female in her search. There are many organisms that select special sites for oviposition, and there must therefore be great diversity in the particular ways they have of homing in on their preferred sites. But rather than examining the sensory or other physiological aspects of oviposition, let us single out the basic adaptive feature of the behavior and concentrate on that.

When *Aedes* oviposits at a water site, is it not essentially "caring" for its young? The eggs are not dropped randomly, but are clustered at the edge of the very habitat that is required for the survival of the larvae. Once the larvae hatch, they must fend for themselves, but they are spared the initial search for water.

Parental care of one type or other is practiced by many animals. Among insects, it is commonplace to find that the adults deposit their eggs on the particular food-plant or other environment required by the larvae. Since metamorphosis is widespread among insects, and since the diets of the larva and adult are often radically different, it is not unexpected that mechanisms should have evolved by which one stage assumes, as it were, the responsibility for minimizing the efforts required of the other for finding its own special environment. And it is not surprising that this responsibility should have fallen upon the adult, since this is the more vigorous stage, capable of bridging distances by straight trajectory in flight.

In some organisms the young are left to themselves from the very outset. Such is the case in many invertebrate animals that are aquatic throughout their life and that shed their gametes and allow fertilization to take place in the water around them. In these organisms there is usually very high mortality among the young, which is compensated by a prodigious reproductive potential. When palolo worms (*Leodice*) swim to the surface waters once a year to spawn, the gametes released, and the zygotes eventually formed, must number in the countless billions. Yet the number of worms that reach maturity is probably not much different from that of the parent generation. One could probably stretch the definition of parental care a bit and say that even *Leodice* shows a certain amount of it. The adult worms, you will recall, live on the ocean bottom. The larvae, by contrast, are planktonic and dwell in the surface waters. When the adults (actually just their rear ends) come to the surface to spawn, are they not essentially returning to the larval habitat and giving the young a proper start?

It would be erroneous to generalize from the above that parental care is most highly developed in organisms in which young and adults inhabit different environments. The exact opposite is sometimes the case. Nowhere is parental care more evident than in social animals. We need not elaborate the obvious case—man himself. In insect societies, including those of termites, ants, bees, and wasps, the young are raised by the adults through their entire development.

There is yet another way we could look at parental care. In many animals, notably those with internal fertilization, the zygote is often retained within the female and nourished by her through the early phases of embryonic development. The young are thereby provided with food and shelter during that part of their life when they are usually most vulnerable. Many species do not necessarily retain the egg within the female for any prolonged period of time after mating, but they deposit the egg with an endowment of yolk, so that the embryo is still actually nourished at the mother's expense. *Aedes,* like other insects, has yolk-laden eggs. The blood meal is the female's way of procuring the necessary nutrient to manufacture yolk. Birds and reptiles are two other groups with richly endowed eggs.

As we mentioned before, animals that incubate their embryos internally, or that lay eggs rich in yolk, are as a rule also those that copulate and have internal fertilization. We also pointed out that organisms that copulate must devote a portion of their adult lives to the active search for a mate, and we inquired about the special adaptations required in order that such organisms may afford, as it were, the necessary leisure for courtship. Let us look into this question of "leisure time" a little further.

Continuous vs. Discontinuous Feeding

Consider yourselves for a moment. On the average, a human being eats three meals per day, which takes relatively little of his time. During most of his waking hours he is free to perform other chores. Let us for the sake of argument define "leisure time" as that amount of time that an organism has available for tasks other than feeding. We immediately recognize that there are enormous differences among animals as regards the percent allocation of their time to feeding.

On the one hand there are animals such as tapeworms and nematodes, as well as nonanimal forms such as bacteria, which live in their food source and are virtually continuous feeders. For them, leisure time literally amounts to none at all. Obviously, it cannot be said that the possession of leisure time is a prerequisite for biological success, since both bacteria and nematodes are among the most successful organisms in the world today. One is hard pressed to think of an ecological niche that cannot at one time or other support at least some sorts of bacteria. Nematodes likewise, both as free-living and parasitic forms, have penetrated virtually every conceivable environment containing organic matter. By sheer weight of numbers they vie even with the insects. But there are certain things that neither bacteria nor nematodes can do. Both of these organisms can lead an active existence *only* as long as they remain with their food source. If they are deprived of food, they either decline and die, or they enter a dormant state (diapause) from which they do not emerge until the environment once again has food to offer. Bacterial spores, and the eggs of nematodes, are the usual stages in which these organisms are inactive. Since they never store nutrients in any considerable amounts, they must bring their metabolic machinery to a halt as soon as food becomes unavailable, otherwise they would quickly die. In a dormant state there is obviously very little that an organism can do. Neither bacteria nor nematodes are notable for their behavioral diversity.

Let us now contrast these organisms with those that do have leisure time. The adult *Aedes* is one of them. We do not really know exactly how much time mosquitoes devote to feeding, but judging from their habits in captivity it is even less time than we ourselves spend at it. A mosquito is therefore free most of the time to pursue other activities. For the male the principal one is the search and subsequent mating of the female. For the female there is also courtship and mating, but in addition there is the important task of finding oviposition sites. We have already discussed the adaptive significance of both of these activities, and have become aware of the complexity of behavior that goes into the performance of each. Let us now examine these activities as being the special privilege of species with leisure time.

What is it about the adult *Aedes* that enables it to be a discontinuous feeder? Most obvious are the special adaptive refinements of its digestive tract. When *Aedes* feeds, whether it be on blood or on sugary fluids, the amount of liquid ingested exceeds by far the immediate demands of the animal. The two capacious compartments of the gut, the large diverticulum of the fore-gut and the mid-gut (Fig. 1–6B), act as reservoirs for the storage of the vast amounts of quickly gathered liquid food, which is then drawn upon in the interval between meals. During its periods of leisure time, a mosquito is therefore by no means operating under starvation conditions, since it is living off the excess provided by the last meal. It can remain fully active.

When *Aedes* feeds, its abdomen swells notably (Fig. 1–4). One might have thought that such swelling would be impossible in an animal that lives within an indistensible cuticular casing. But although the cuticle of the adult *Aedes* is indeed indistensible, it is nevertheless adapted to accommodate fluctuations in body volume. This is because the abdominal cuticle is not a uniform shell of even thickness, but consists of a series of dorsal and ventral plates hinged to one another by folded strips of thin cuticular membrane. When the animal gorges itself, it is these membranes that unfold (they do not stretch), allowing the abdomen to swell. (The membranes are so thin that one can see some of the inner organs through them when they are unfolded in the replete mosquito: Fig. 1–4.)

The possession of a distensible abdomen is also of importance for *Aedes* in another respect. As the eggs develop inside the female, they are endowed gradually with increasing amounts of yolk and they enlarge accordingly, so that by the time the female is ready to oviposit, her abdomen is once again conspicuously swollen. Were it not for her ability to withhold a sizable egg batch, she would have to lay eggs one at a time as they are formed within her, and would not be able to retain them for deposition in clusters. A trip to a water hole would be required each time an egg is formed, which would enormously increase the female's investment of energy per egg laid. The possession of a distensible abdomen (Fig. 2–2) is thus to be viewed as an important adaptive feature since, by enabling the animal to feed discontinuously, it provides for leisure in which time-consuming activities such as courtship and the search for oviposition sites can be carried out. Needless to say, leisure time can also be used in the search for food. Time is required for *Aedes* to seek a human host, just as time is required to find a mate. The ability to accommodate large intestinal loads in little time has enabled insects to evolve highly specialized food habits.

The overwhelming majority of vertebrates are also discontinuous feeders. Their stomach serves for the accumulation of rapidly gathered food, and their soft body wall, devoid of cuticle, offers no insurmountable resistance and yields by distension whenever the animal gorges itself (think of a snake, bulging with an ingested rodent). A distensible body also makes possible the production of large eggs, or even the prolonged internal incubation of embryos (think of a pregnant mammal). In short, there are remarkable parallels in the adaptive achievements of vertebrates and insects. Both are discontinuous feeders, with ample leisure time at their disposal, and both have evolved highly complex behavior patterns by which their leisure time is, so to speak, put to adaptive use. It is no small wonder that texts on animal behavior are filled with descriptions of the elaborate feeding, courtship, and reproductive behavior of insects and vertebrates. There is very little that is usually said about nematodes. All of these generalizations are not, of course, without exception. The larvae of many insects, and particularly

Fig. 2-2. "Replete" workers of the ant *Myrmecocystus*. The abdomens are enormously swollen with stored food. The remainder of the colony obtains food by regurgitation from these repletes.

herbivorous ones, spend virtually all their active time feeding. But their adults usually do not.

Let us return to nematodes and re-examine them in the light of what was just said about insects and vertebrates. A nematode has one outstanding characteristic in common with an insect. It possesses an indistensible body cuticle. Like insects, nematodes cannot grow unless they shed their cuticle periodically by molting. But unlike insects, their cuticle is fairly uniform around the entire body and lacks the kind of folded membranes that enable *Aedes*' abdomen to swell with food or eggs (Fig. 2–3). A nematode is literally straitjacketed, and this accounts for many of the peculiarities of its way of life. Being incapable of gorging itself intermittently, it must rely on a more or less continuous intake of food. This is why a nematode must remain with its food source if it is to lead an active life. One might say that the lack of locomotory organs such as legs and wings in a nematode reflects the lack of time in which to use them. There is also no way a nematode can accumulate sizable egg clusters within its body. Nematodes do lay enormous numbers of eggs in a lifetime, but they lay them more or less continuously rather than intermittently in batches (there are again exceptions to this rule).

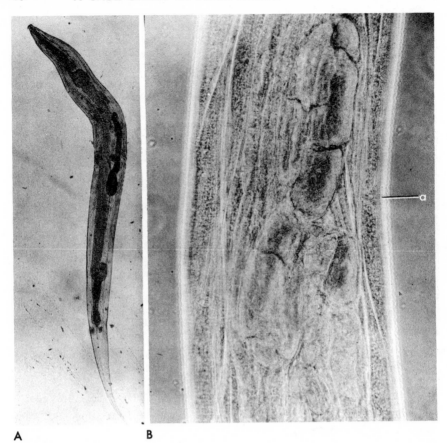

A   B

Fig. 2-3. A: A nematode (*Enterobius vermicularis*) parasitic in the intestine of man. B: Enlarged portion of same, showing cuticle, a.

Since the eggs of nematodes are laid by the parents in the very food source they inhabit, one would expect young nematodes to share the parental environment as well as the parental diet. One would expect them to be generally adapted like the parents, and to resemble them in all major respects except size. In short, one would *not* expect nematodes to have a metamorphosis comparable to that of insects. All of this turns out to be essentially true for free-living nematodes. Their young are indeed no more than miniature versions of the adults. But parasitic nematodes sometimes have complex life cycles, with larvae that live in unique habitats of their own. In adaptation to their special habitat, the larvae sometimes have distinct features not shared with the adults, and in the life cycle of these worms there is therefore, in the very sense of the word, a metamorphosis. Still, the parents are continuous feeders, and as a rule (pinworms are a peculiar exception) they do not depart from their own habitat in an active search for a special environment in which to oviposit. Completion of the life cycle is much more a matter of chance than it is in *Aedes,* but parasitic nematodes effectively compensate for the risks involved by producing enormous numbers of eggs. A single female hookworm, for instance, may produce over 10,000 eggs per day, as compared with the few hundred laid by an *Aedes* in a lifetime. (Incidentally, egg laying is a continuous business for a hookworm; never more than 5 percent of the daily output of eggs can be counted within the body of the female at any one time. This is obviously of significance in connection with what we said earlier about a nematode's inability to accumulate growing quantities of eggs or any other material within itself.) In some parasitic nematodes the larvae inhabit a second host distinct from the parental one. The larval host may be associated in its behavior with the parental host, and this may reduce some of the risks involved in completing the life cycle. For instance, the adults of *Wuchereria bancrofti* (which causes the dreaded elephantiasis) live in humans, but the larvae mature in female mosquitoes, which transmit them among humans through the blood meal.

From all the preceding it is evident that nematodes and insects illustrate two rather distinct modes of life. Our choice of the concept of leisure time as a basis for comparing and contrasting these two ways of life was purely arbitrary. We could have singled out any other concept (for example, the reproductive potential, or the water impermeability of the integument) and reasoned from there. This might possibly have added new dimensions to our discussion by bringing into perspective adaptive features that were overlooked by our present approach, but probably the over-all feeling with which we would have emerged about the relative adaptive merits of two ways of life would have been no different. Neither way of life is "better" than the other. Neither type of animal is more "highly" adapted than the other. Living within a straitjacket, or possessing an adjustable belt, are simply two alternatives to adaptive success, each with potentials and restrictions that are uniquely their own.

DEVELOPMENT

In the first chapter we learned that the development of *Aedes* was marked by four definite stages: egg, larva, pupa, and adult. We raised the question as to whether this type of development is not a very roundabout way of achieving adult and sexual competency, and questioned the adaptive significance of this type of life cycle. Let us now examine each of the developmental stages individually, and look for similar or dissimilar types of development in other forms.

The Egg

Eggs in protective envelopes are laid by many species of animals, and not only by terrestrial forms such as insects. However, there are countless modifications of eggs, both structural and physiological, unique to particular groups of organisms or even to individual species. We will begin by analyzing in some detail the significance of special adaptations in the egg of *Aedes*.

The shell

One of the first things we noted about the *Aedes* egg was the shell itself. It is tough and for this reason offers protection to the enclosed embryo. But it is also protective in more subtle ways. We noted in passing that the shell in opaque; it is, in fact, black. When we remember that the egg is laid on solid objects just above the water line, the dark coloration takes on significance. First, since the substrate bearing the egg is itself likely to be colored, it is clear that a white egg would be less adequately camouflaged than a dark one. Second, and probably more significant, the pigmentation may serve to protect the animal against excessive sunlight. Admittedly, this has not been demonstrated experimentally, but excessive sunlight—and particularly the ultraviolet components thereof—are known to be harmful to living cells. Since the diapausing embryo of *Aedes* may at times have to remain exposed for weeks to sunlight before the rising water level finally triggers hatching, a transparent shell might offer only insufficient shielding.

The reason that the egg, with the tiny diapausing larva within it, can remain exposed to air for weeks and even months without drying up is because the shell is virtually water impermeable. However, during the first one to three days after deposition, the egg will die if deprived of moisture. This is the period during which the embryo undergoes active development, and the requirement for water probably reflects the fact that the egg, which at this time must maintain a moist surface to permit proper respiratory exchange, is prone to desiccation. Once the embryo has developed and diapause sets in, respiration declines sharply and a virtually impermeable egg shell can then be tolerated.

For the sake of comparison, let us examine another egg shell—that of the bird. How does it resemble and how does it differ from that of *Aedes*? Pigmentation is quite common in bird eggs. Camouflage is usually involved, and many striking cases could be cited of eggs with color patterns that blend beautifully with that of the substrate on which they are laid. The pigment may also protect the eggs from sunlight, although the unpigmented calcified shell may in itself be a rather good shield. Birds that nest in darkness frequently lay white eggs.

Birds do not, as does *Aedes*, cement their eggs to the substrate. This would make it impossible for them to revolve the eggs in the nests, as many of them do periodically to ensure that the developing embryo is evenly exposed to the warmth supplied by the incubating mother and also to prevent damaging adhesions from taking place in some of the embryonic membranes. But there are adaptations that ensure that an egg will stay in place. In nesting birds, an appropriate trough for the eggs is of course provided by the nest itself. However, there are birds that lay their eggs in exposed places such as cliffs. The eggs of these birds are typically plump at one end and sharply pointed at the other. Any tendency to displace them will cause them to roll in a tight circle, rather than in a straight line like a ball (Fig. 2–4).

The shell of a bird egg is porous, permitting free diffusion of respiratory gases across it. Since in the absence of diapause a high respiratory demand is maintained throughout development, the porosity of the egg remains unchanged. This porosity results in a continual unavoidable water loss, which over an entire incubation period may amount to over 20 percent of the original water content of the egg. Some birds are reported to reduce this water loss by sprinkling their eggs occasionally with water brought in the bill. This may also prevent overheating.

The shell is not necessarily evenly porous throughout. There are usually more pores on the blunt end than elsewhere on the egg. Beneath the shell at this blunt end there is an air space into which projects the head and bill of the maturing embryo. Once the lungs become functional, the animal is optimally positioned with its head in air, beneath the most porous portion of the shell.

The shell need not become a total waste after development is complete. A young chick after hatching turns and begins to peck at the shell. The intake of shell not only provides the young animal with a potentially utilizable

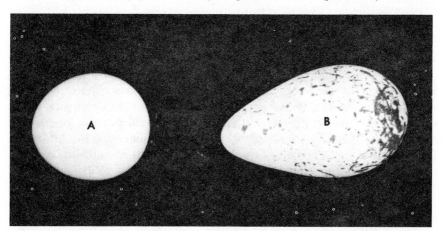

Fig. 2-4. A: Egg of the great horned owl (*Bubo virginianus*). The bird nests in trees and the egg is white. B: Pointed egg of a thick-billed murre (*Uria lomvia*), which lays eggs in open sites on cliffs. (Eggs courtesy of Neal Smith, Cornell University.)

mineral source, but also serves as the first grinding material in the animal's gizzard.

Other modifications of the avian egg could be mentioned, but the present discussion should satisfy the reader that the hard covering on the surface of the developing embryo not only serves to protect the animal against mechanical damage, but contributes to many different aspects of the animal's early development. The possibility that adaptations serve multiple functions should never be overlooked. Let us now consider the egg from a somewhat different standpoint.

Egg size

It is sometimes taken for granted that adaptations promoting increased egg production are invariably at an evolutionary premium. A moment's reflection should suffice to rule out the validity of this generalization. As we have already mentioned, there is enormous variation in the reproductive potential of species, and adaptive success is by no means always correlated with high egg production. As a general rule it may be said that the number of eggs produced by a species reflects the percent mortality suffered by that species in the completion of its life cycle. Species that lay enormous numbers of eggs are relatively ill-adapted to withstand the hazards of survival, and they suffer high mortality, mostly in the earlier stages of development. We have already seen how parasitic nematodes compensate for the risks involved in the completion of their often tortuously complicated life cycles by laying thousands or even millions of eggs per female. Many other parasites fall in the same category. Organisms that lay few eggs have young that develop in relatively safe environments, or else they are adaptively equipped to withstand better the threats to their existence.

It is common for organisms that produce only few eggs to produce relatively large ones. The large size is indicative of substantial yolk endowment, and this is, of course, one of the ways that organisms can maximize the chance of their offspring's survival early in life. The young are spared the initial search for food, and by the time they hatch have already outgrown what could potentially be the most vulnerable stage of their existence.

We emphasized earlier that endowment with yolk as a rule occurs only in organisms that show some form of courtship behavior, whereby gamete fertilization is given a high chance of occurrence. It would obviously be uneconomical for an organism to endow all eggs with yolk if only a small fraction will eventually be fertilized. In our earlier discussion of "parental care" these generalizations were illustrated with examples. But there are exceptions to the rules.

Not all organisms that court and mate produce large yolk-laden eggs. Humans, for example, produce a very small egg once a month. But the embryo, as in all mammals, remains with the mother and is nourished directly by her. This obviates the need for an initial lump deposition of yolk in the egg itself.

There are also some species that produce relatively few eggs despite their complete lack of courtship or mating behavior. To this category belong the green hydras. These fresh-water coelenterates are hermaphroditic; that is, testes and ovaries may develop in the same individual (Fig. 2–5). The number of gametes produced by a hydra is ordinarily insufficient to account for the maintenance of the species. But the animal does not reproduce by sexual means alone. It can reproduce generation after generation through the asexual process of budding. When sexuality ensues, cross-fertilization (that is, sperm from one individual fertilizing eggs of another) stands a frequent chance of occurrence only if individuals are relatively closely spaced. The ability to reproduce asexually is obviously an adaptive safeguard for a species in which successful sexual reproduction is dependent on a high population density. One might add that green hydras are not self-sterile, which means that sperm from one individual can fertilize the eggs of that same individual. Thus, even a single hydra with no close neighbors can have its eggs fertilized. But self-fertilization does not entail the same potential for genetic recombination as does cross-fertilization, hence it is not really a true substitute for the latter. It is to be viewed merely as a safeguard or "last resort" that prevents total wastage of gametes in the occasional isolated individual.

Hermaphroditism is common in many other invertebrates, including planarians, tapeworms, flukes, mollusks, and annelids. In many tapeworms, (Fig. 3–2), which are likely to find themselves confined singly in the host without a mate, self-fertilization can and does occur. But in other hermaphrodites, self-fertilization may never occur, and may, in fact, be impossible for anatomical reasons. In many planarians, earthworms, and snails, each individual can have both testes and ovaries, but the organisms copulate in pairs. A two-way reciprocal insemination takes place whereby the sperm of one individual are delivered to the eggs

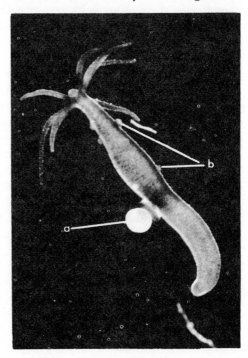

Fig. 2-5. A green *Hydra*: a, ovary; b, testes.

of the other, and vice versa. Cross-fertilization is thus assured. Offhand one might imagine that reciprocal insemination of this sort is a rather expedient approach to sexual reproduction. Why then is hermaphroditism so conspicuously absent in many dominant groups of animals (for example, arthropods and vertebrates)? Evidently, under certain circumstances—which the reader might attempt to determine—there has been strong selection in favor of bisexuality.

If we examine the question of the size and number of eggs produced by animals, and at the same time consider the type of environments they inhabit, we notice an interesting correlation. Marine animals, and particularly the invertebrates, usually produce tiny eggs in large numbers. This holds true for many annelids, mollusks, echinoderms, and others. Fresh-water animals, by contrast, produce relatively few large eggs. Why should it be of selective advantage in fresh water to lay eggs rich in yolk? We can get a clue to the answer by slightly rephrasing the question. Why should it be of selective advantage in fresh water to hatch from the egg at a relatively advanced and hence more vigorous stage of development?

The larvae of marine invertebrates as a rule are tiny and weak ciliated forms that drift in the surface waters and feed on plankton. They are small for the simple reason that the eggs from which they stem are poor in yolk, thus forcing them at an early stage to embark upon an active food-gathering existence. Such weak swimmers would be powerless against the currents of rivers, which would simply sweep them downstream. In the course of evolution, when marine animals colonized the fresh waters, the route of invasion must have been through the estuaries and up into rivers and streams. Possession of a tiny ciliated larva was incompatible with survival in the new habitat, and the only forms that managed to invade it were those with larvae strong enough to withstand currents from the very moment of hatching.

A lobster and its fresh-water counterpart, a crayfish, provide interesting examples in this connection. A lobster produces several thousand small eggs per season, from which hatch tiny larvae that swim in the plankton and feed upon it. A crayfish may produce no more than a few dozen eggs, but they are considerably larger than those of the lobster. The eggs are attached to the underside of the mother's abdomen, and the young, which on hatching are already about 1 centimeter long, remain with the mother through their first molt and do not depart until several days later. They resemble tiny adults in appearance, and from the outset lead much the same bottom-dwelling life.

Other examples could be cited. Marine snails and bivalve mollusks as a rule produce eggs in large numbers and of small size. Their larvae are planktonic. Fresh-water species usually lay fewer and larger eggs. The young frequently hatch as small adults, having passed their entire larval development within the yolk-laden egg. In some fresh-water mussels the emerging larvae are relatively small, but they are parasitic on fish, which provide them with a "cheap" means of dispersal while at the same time ensuring that they are not at the mercy of currents.

One should not conclude from the preceding that the only adaptive prerequisite for colonization of fresh water was the possession of vigorous larvae. The story is a good deal more complex than that. There is at least one important group of animals, the cephalopod mollusks (squid, octopus, and relatives), that has not given rise to a single fresh-water representative despite the fact that the hatchlings are rather large and powerful swimmers. Fresh water differs from the oceans in more respects than one. Reduced salinity and buoyancy, plus relatively wide temperature fluctuations, are just a few additional factors to which marine organisms had to adapt in their evolutionary transition to fresh water. We will have more to say of this later.

It is worth noting here, however, that some of the other topics considered earlier in connection with reproduction can now be viewed somewhat differently than before, namely in terms of the adaptive requisites of special environments. For instance, we mentioned that endowment of eggs with yolk is more likely to occur in animals that have internal fertilization than in those that rely on the rather risky prospects of chance fertilization in the water around them. Should one therefore expect internal fertilization to be more widespread in fresh-water forms than in marine forms? Courtship, mating, yolk endowment of eggs, internal incubation of the young—all of these could now be re-evaluated in terms of their relative adaptive fitness in the two major types of aquatic habitats.

The preceding discussion raises some interesting questions regarding the evolutionary colonization of land. Biologists generally agree that life arose in the oceans. Fresh-water and terrestrial organisms are therefore *all* ultimately derived from marine forms. This presents two possibilities as regards the evolutionary ancestry of terrestrial animals. Either they arose directly from marine forms, or else they were derived from fresh-water forms that in turn had marine ancestors. On the basis of what has been said about the special demands for survival in fresh water and in the oceans, one might now ask, which types of animal—fresh water or marine—were likely to have been best adapted to make the transition to a terrestrial habitat? In other words, which of the two would have had to undergo the *least* adaptive change to succeed in colonizing land? Egg size alone is likely to have been an important factor, although a great many others were undoubtedly involved.

Diapause

Diapause—a state of arrested growth—is found in the life cycle of many insects and other animals, and not necessarily always in the egg stage. In *Aedes,* the adaptive significance of diapause is twofold. First, the mosquito is provided with a stage in its life cycle in which prolonged drought conditions can be withstood with relative safety. And second, since hatching at the end of diapause is triggered by the reavailability of water, vast numbers of larvae in any one area are likely to begin developing simultaneously, ensuring the eventual emergence of appropriately dense adult mating populations.

In other animals, diapause has comparable significance. The condition of virtual metabolic arrest characteristic of diapause conveys upon an organism an unusually high resistance to environmental stress. Thus diapause enables organisms to survive the temporary inclemencies of an inconstant environment, while at the same time making possible the adaptive synchronization of their life cycles to the prevailing environmental fluctuations.

There are virtually no regions on this earth that can be said to have a year-round constant environment. The greatest over-all stability is found in the oceans. On land, and in the inland waters, there are seasonal temperature fluctuations that far exceed those in the oceans, and that become more and more pronounced the farther one moves from the equator. But even in the tropics, where there are no seasons in the strict sense of the word, the availability of rainfall may vary enormously, and one often recognizes "rainy" or "dry" seasons. Diapause is thus most widespread in fresh-water and terrestrial forms, and it is usually geared to coincide with periods of unfavorable temperature or low water availability.

In the colder subtropics, for instance, there are virtually no insects to be seen during the snowy winter months. Many of them are in diapause, either in the egg, larval, or pupal stages. (Some also overwinter as inactive adults, but we do not speak of adults as being in diapause, since the term is used to refer to a condition of arrested *growth*, and adults have already completed theirs). What determines the onset of diapause in the fall, and what triggers its cessation in the spring? Only relatively few species have been studied in great detail but, as might be expected, the critical factors are usually environmental temperature or daylength. Certain moths of the family Saturniidae overwinter as diapausing pupae. The caterpillars spin their cocoons in the late summer or early fall and pupate inside them; then as the temperature drops diapause sets in. Adult development within the pupa does not begin until the organism has been exposed to the chilling temperatures of winter. As the temperature rises in early spring, and the days grow longer, the developmental machinery is set into motion, and when the adult eventually emerges, it does so in proper synchrony with its mates, and with the developing foliage of the food plant of its future young (the plants themselves were in diapause during the winter). Evidently, the pupa must be capable in some fashion of gauging, as it were, the advent of spring. It is known that the onset of adult development is triggered by a hormone produced by certain cells in the pupal brain. But how does the brain "know" when to begin secreting its hormone? Much remains to be learned about this topic, but it appears that the brain itself is capable of "measuring" the changing environmental conditions. In some saturniids, temperature is the critical factor. Others rely on the change in daylength. In the latter there is even a small transparent window on the cuticle of the pupal head through which the brain can "see" and thereby "measure" the changing length of day. One wonders in what subtle physiological way living systems can actually make such measurements. In *Aedes*, for instance, we do not really know exactly how water acts to break diapause and trigger hatching.

We mentioned earlier that the relatively great temperature instability of fresh waters must have been an important factor affecting the evolutionary colonization of this habitat by marine forms. Sponges provide an interesting example in this connection. They are primitively and predominantly marine organisms, but they have produced a single large family that lives in fresh water. Some of these fresh-water sponges can survive conditions of freezing such as none of their marine relatives ever have to face. But they do not survive these conditions as fully grown sponges. When the environment becomes unfavorable, special ameboid cells, known as archeocytes, collect in discrete areas in the sponge tissue, where each aggregate becomes enrobed within a membrane. The resulting capsules are called gemmules. The tissues of the parent sponge may then disintegrate, leaving the encapsulated gemmules behind. The gemmules then enter a period of diapause, during which they can withstand the chilling temperatures of winter. As conditions once again become warmer, they emerge from diapause and differentiate into sponges. The specific mechanisms that induce and terminate diapause remain unknown in most of these sponges. In certain species of temperate regions, gemmule formation may be an annual phenomenon, coincident with the advent of the cold winter season. Some of these sponges have become so completely adapted to the annual recurrence of winter that their gemmules *require* previous exposure to winter temperatures before they can develop. Such gemmules are convenient material for experimental studies on growth and development, and investigators have found that if they wish gemmules to develop in the laboratory, they must first expose them to an artificial winter in a refrigerator. In the saturniid moths mentioned earlier there is also an obligatory dependence on the chills of winter. Without it, diapause cannot be broken subsequently by the advent of spring.

The Larva

The larva of *Aedes* does precisely what one expects a larva to do—it feeds. It is the only true growing stage in the life cycle, and virtually its entire existence is geared to the procurement of food. In a sense, the larva does more than provide for itself. By the time it pupates, it has accumulated a substantial surplus of reserves, and this surplus, plus whatever is salvaged from the remainder of the larva, is eventually utilized in the formation of the adult. In some insects, as for example in the saturniid moths mentioned above, the adult never feeds. The larva in these species must provide not only for the development of the adult, but also for the subsequent maintenance of the adult's metabolism, and even for the eggs eventually laid. Thus, advanced provision is essentially made by each crop of larvae for the incipient stages of the next larval generation.

We could go on belaboring animal larvae and their food habits. For insects alone this would require an entire book. *Aedes* is actually a rather exceptional insect larva, not so much because it lives in water (many orders of insects have independently evolved species with aquatic larvae), but because it is a filter feeder. Filter feeding is primarily a characteristic of plankton-sifting oceanic forms, and insects are almost entirely absent from the oceans.

The majority of insect larvae share the terrestrial habitat of their parents, and, since the bulk of living matter on land is comprised of plants, most are herbivorous. But there are many insect larvae, both terrestrial and aquatic, that are carnivorous, feeding primarily on their fellow insects. The enormous diversity of larval food habits—habits that often differ radically from those of the corresponding adults—illustrates, perhaps better than anything else, the extent to which insects exploited the evolutionary potential of metamorphosis.

If we wanted to compare insect larvae to those of other animals, we would quickly realize that our search for larval types might most fruitfully be conducted in the oceans. In both fresh water and on land we would be hard pressed to find animals with young sufficiently dissimilar from their adults to justify being called larvae. There are, of course, exceptions, the Amphibia—with larvae such as tadpoles—being an obvious one. But disregarding insects and Amphibia, it is certainly true that neither on land nor in inland waters is there to be found anything approaching the wealth of larval types displayed in the oceans. This raises some questions. We have already speculated on the absence of larvae in fresh water, and argued that for survival in that habitat it is of selective advantage to compress larval stages into the prehatching phases of development. But what about the general absence of larvae on land? Why, for instance, do many amphibians have larvae, and why have free-living larval stages been suppressed in their terrestrial descendents—that is, in the reptiles, birds, and mammals? If the terrestrial habitat selected against the retention of larvae by vertebrates, why did it favor the evolutionary acquisition of larvae by insects? These questions are not easy to answer, and they require the concurrent evaluation of a variety of adaptive considerations (for example, the relative susceptibility of vertebrates and insects to desiccation).

Let us turn to the abundance of larvae in the oceans. Most of these larvae are planktonic. If we were to collect a sample of plankton by dragging a fine-meshed net through oceanic surface waters, we would find that the majority of planktonic organisms are not animals at all but plants. Microscopic algae (Fig. 2–6), which form the bulk of plankton, are the major food source of the oceans. Directly or indirectly, these algae support all marine animal life, and it is only appropriate that they should be called the "grass of the oceans." In addition to algae, the plankton sample would contain a diversity of crustaceans, and the remainder would consist largely of an assortment of mostly tiny and often bizarre larvae.

These larvae belong to a rather impressive array of animals, including many annelids, arthropods, mollusks, ectoprocts, endoprocts, echinoderms, tunicates, and others. If we took an over-all glance at this entire complex of animals, focusing in a general way on their life cycles, we would notice first of all that their larvae, like those of insects and other animals, represent

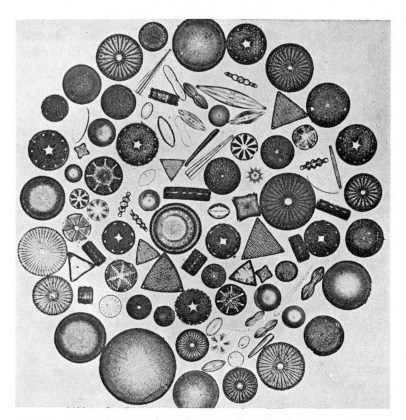

Fig. 2-6. Marine diatoms. These algae form the bulk of plankton. (Courtesy of General Biological Supply House, Inc., Chicago.)

the growth stage of the life cycle. But beyond this basic similarity with insects, we would be most struck by some of the dissimilarities. For instance, in sharp contrast to adult insects, which have legs and wings and can do a good deal of moving about, the marine forms lead a rather stationary life as adults. Some of them, such as many oysters, mussels, tunicates, endoprocts, ectoprocts, and some echinoderms, are anchored to the ocean floor and do not move at all. Others, such as starfish, snails, and many annelids, are not strictly sessile, but they lack the means for quick travel and in actual fact spend much or all of their adult life confined to relatively small territories. The larvae of these animals, living suspended in plankton and drifting with the currents, may cover distances much greater than those ever traveled by the adults. In short, *dispersal* in these forms is accomplished, not by the adults as in insects, but by the larvae.

Dispersal is a most important adaptive phenomenon. Imagine what would happen if each new generation were bound to grow up in the immediate vicinity of the parents. A condition of overcrowding would eventually ensue, in which food shortages, as well as a variety of other stress conditions that commonly arise on crowding, would impose a high mortality rate upon the population. Evidently, the possession of a motile stage in the life cycle capable of migrating to potentially more favorable ground elsewhere is an adaptive asset to a species.

Is there any significance in the fact that dispersal in insects is by the adults, whereas in marine forms it is most often by the larvae? There are several possible approaches to answering this question, one of which involves consideration of a basic difference between the terrestrial and marine habitats. In the oceans it is possible for a larva to feed continuously while at the same time being, as it were, "on the move." The "grass of the oceans" is not rooted as are the plants on land, but drifts free as part of the plankton. Any larva drifting with and feeding on plankton is therefore inevitably prone to dispersal.

Since plants on land are by necessity anchored, it is impossible for a terrestrial larva to feed on plants and travel at the same time. It is therefore obviously adaptive for insects to add wings only *after* they are fully grown. Clearly, this is not the only adaptive justification for the flightlessness of the immatures. The reader might attempt to determine in what ways an imaginary insect with winged larvae and flightless adults would be ill-suited for survival. There are many alterations that such an insect would have to undergo in order to be adaptively fit—in fact, once all the compensatory modifications were made, one could probably no longer call it an insect at all!

Dispersal sometimes occurs during a diapausing or otherwise dormant stage of the life cycle. Wind and other natural forces are involved in the dispersal of bacterial spores and of the diapausing eggs of many nematodes.

A whole treatise could be written on the special adaptations that facilitate dispersal by plant seeds.

A most interesting case is provided by the so-called "ballooning" of spiders. These arthropods lack the wings of insects and are therefore confined to the ground. But in some species the young do in fact disperse by taking to the air. They do this in a most peculiar fashion. First, they climb to a prominent outpost, such as the tip of a blade of grass, where they assume a position with their abdomens (which bear the openings of the silk glands) pointing straight up. They then secrete a thread of silk into the air, and eventually, when the thread is long enough, they release their foothold and allow themselves to be carried at the ends of their threads by the wind. Once adrift, they can pull their "sail" back in again by rolling the thread up with their feet, and bring themselves back to earth. Considerable distances can be spanned in this fashion, and there are records of live ballooning spiders having drifted onto ships in mid-ocean.

The Pupa

So far, every feature of *Aedes* that we have chosen to examine, be it of an anatomical, physiological, or behavioral nature, has invariably led us to a comparative consideration of equivalent or alternative features in other organisms. But when faced with the insect pupa, we are at a loss in finding anything that is truly comparable in other animals. The pupa is a uniquely insect feature.

Not even all insects have pupae. In the evolutionarily more ancient insects there is what is known as a "gradual" metamorphosis. A cockroach, for instance, has young that at hatching closely resemble the adults, differing from them in no major way except in the absence of wings and the lack of a functional reproductive system (Fig. 2–7). With each molt the young simply enlarge in size, and no drastic change takes place until the last molt, when fully formed wings appear and reproductive competence is achieved. A young cockroach lives in much the same habitat as the adult, and shares the adult's diet. This kind of development is obviously a far cry from that of *Aedes*.

A pupa is found in those insects with larvae that are conspicuously adapted to a different way of life from the adults. The dissimilarity between larva and adult is so pronounced that a major reorganization is required to transform the one into the other. The pupa provides the "dressing room" in which the change of habit takes place. Flies, mosquitoes, butterflies, moths, beetles, bees, and wasps are but a few of the many types of insects in which there is a "complete" metamorphosis with pupal stage.

What are the respective adaptive merits of gradual and complete metamorphosis? Insects that have complete metamorphosis often exploit two

A   B

Fig. 2-7. The American cockroach (*Periplaneta americana*). The adult (B) differs from the immature (A) in no major way except in the possession of wings and a functional reproductive system. There is no pupal stage, and the species is said to have *gradual* metamorphosis.

entirely different food sources during their development. This is well illustrated by *Aedes*, but many other examples could be cited. Butterflies, for instance, feed on nectar, but their caterpillars as a rule devour leaves, and not necessarily those of the same plants that provide the nectar for the parents. Offhand we might reason that the exploitation of two different food sources by a single animal is bound to have greater adaptive merits than the exploitation of a single food source, simply because it is "safer" for a species not to be overly restricted in its diet. One might argue, for instance, that an animal with a restricted diet is more susceptible to single calamities affecting its food source than one capable of shifting under such circumstances to alternative food sources not affected by the calamity. There is some merit in such argument, but *not* as it applies to insect metamorphosis. For, when we say that an insect exploits two food sources during its development, we do not mean to say that these are *alternative* food sources. The blood meal of the adult *Aedes* is as necessary for the completion of the life cycle as are the bacteria taken by the larvae. The argument does apply when we view the degree of restriction of the diet at any *one* stage in development. Thus it might be said that from an adaptive standpoint it is "safer" for the *Aedes* larva to be capable of feeding on a wide assortment of bacteria than to depend on only a few types. Similarly, a caterpillar feeding on a wide selection of plant leaves might be thought of as leading a potentially less hazardous life than one restricted to a single species of plant. As regards the adult *Aedes* we would then have to say that its almost exclusive dependence on man for a blood meal represents a "dangerous" restriction of its diet. But even this phase of the argument can be turned around, since one could make a good case in many instances for the adaptive advantages of a restricted diet. There are many animals that are surviving most effectively despite highly specialized food habits. Not only do they often depend on just a single dietary item, but the item may be a rather scarce one. Such animals have evolved highly refined sensory faculties that enable them to locate the scarce item on which they subsist, and they often spend a good deal of "leisure time" finding it. True, they may be thought of as having become dangerously overspecialized. But they also profit often from a relative freedom from competition, since they may be very much alone in exploiting the particular food source of their choice.

We have not as yet answered our previous question about the adaptive significance of complete metamorphosis. There is not a single pat answer that can be given. Complete metamorphosis may provide an insect with an opportunity for exploiting two separate and sometimes scarce food sources, neither of which might in itself suffice to maintain the species in large numbers. Also, and probably most important, it may enable a species to maintain a continuing life cycle geared to the consecutive exploitation of food sources with different seasonal peaks of abundance. A caterpillar may be specialized to feed on the young emergent shoots of a plant in early spring; the adult butterflies may then feed on the nectar of another plant blooming later in the summer. There are other aspects of metamorphosis that could be considered in this context, but further elaboration is left to the reader. Consider the fact, for example, that most organisms that metamorphose, including even many with greatly dissimilar immature and mature forms, make a gradual transition from larva to adult instead of relying on an interposed pupal stage. Think of the gradual transformation of a tadpole to a frog. The tadpole begins to grow legs long before it is ready to assume the terrestrial mode of life in which it will use them. Would it not be "better" to retain the legless streamlined shape of the early tadpole throughout the aquatic phase of development, and to allow the transformation to the adult frog to take place all at once in a special pupal stage? Why are pupae absent in organisms other than insects? Is it that such organisms could gain no adaptive advantage from the possession of a pupal stage? Or is it that they lack certain adaptive prerequisites without which the evolutionary acquisition of a pupa becomes improbable or impossible? Or is a combination of many factors involved? Are these questions perhaps entirely the wrong ones to ask? If so, how could they be rephrased and made more meaningful?

One additional example of metamorphosis will be given, because it involves a peculiar case in which a pronounced changeover from larva to adult occurs in a surprisingly short time. The case in point is that of a group of animals not well known to most people—the tunicates, or sea squirts as they are sometimes called. These animals are immobile throughout their adult life. They were once thought to be mollusks because they possess two siphons, one for the intake of plankton-laden water, and the other for the subsequent expulsion of residual water. But once their larval stages were discovered, it became clear that these animals really belong to the Chordata, the same phylum to which we ourselves belong.

The life cycle of a typical tunicate, *Molgula,* will serve as an example of the group. The animals spawn and fertilization takes place in the water. The fertilized eggs develop in a matter of hours into a small free-swimming larva, called a tadpole. This larva has a notochord and all other characters necessary to classify it as a chordate. It is a highly complex little organism, equipped with light-sensitive organ, a well-developed tail, plus brain, heart, gut, balancing organ, mouth, and anus (Fig. 2–8).

The young tadpole swims about by lashing movements of its tail, grazing on plankton as it moves along. Eventually, it settles on a favorable site by attaching itself with two discs at its front end, and it metamorphoses into the adult. The tail is resorbed first. This process can be nearly completed within 15 minutes. The remainder of the entire transformation from tadpole to adult takes no more than a few additional hours.

Tunicates illustrate the rather common type of marine life cycle with sessile adult and free-swimming larva. Both adult and larva feed on plankton. We cannot therefore generalize on the basis of what was learned previously from insects—that metamorphosis invariably involves the transformation from one feeding type into another. In tunicates, the tadpole is to be viewed as a locomotory stage adapted specifically for dispersal. In this respect a tunicate tadpole differs obviously from that of a frog. The reader might attempt on his own to draw some comparisons between the metamorphosis of an insect, a frog, and a tunicate.

The Adult

Much about the adult has already been said or implied in the preceding sections of our discussion. We focused on the feeding habits of adults and considered the relative adaptive merits of continuous and discontinuous

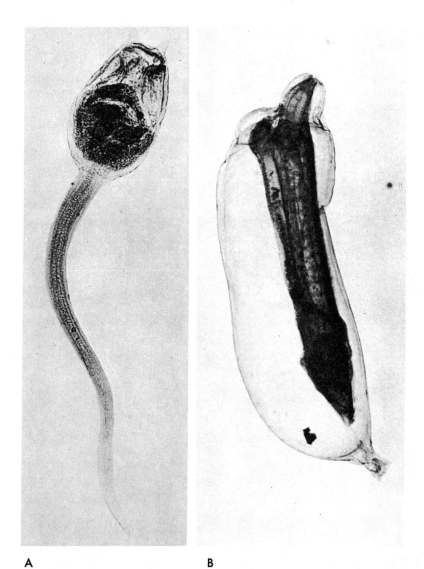

A   B

Fig. 2-8. Larval (A) and adult (B) tunicate. The adult is ordinarily sessile, but has been torn at its base in this stained individual. (Courtesy of General Biological Supply House, Inc., Chicago.)

feeding. We examined spawning, courtship, and mating activities. We looked at the reproductive potential of species and saw how some lay eggs by the millions, others lay few large ones, and still others incubate their young internally.

We tend to think of an adult as the *reproductive* stage in the life cycle, and this is actually our criterion for defining what we mean by adult. But let us examine the following life cycle and see what this does to our definition.

Aurelia is a common marine jellyfish (Fig. 2–9). Together with the green hydras mentioned earlier, it belongs to the phylum Coelenterata. Its life cycle is considerably more complex than that of *Hydra* since it involves a metamorphosis. The sexually competent stage of the life cycle is the typical jellyfish or *medusa.* Eggs and sperm are shed into the water and fertilization is external. The zygote develops into a small ciliated larva called a *planula,* which drifts about until it eventually settles on a solid substrate and grows into the next developmental stage, the *polyp.* The polyp is a cylindrical body attached at its base and bearing on its distal surface a mouth surrounded by tentacles. It resembles *Hydra* and is in fact built in much the same way. The polyp completes the life cycle by forming medusae. One polyp does not transform into a single medusa, but gives rise to many of them through asexual budding. The tiny medusae are sloughed off from

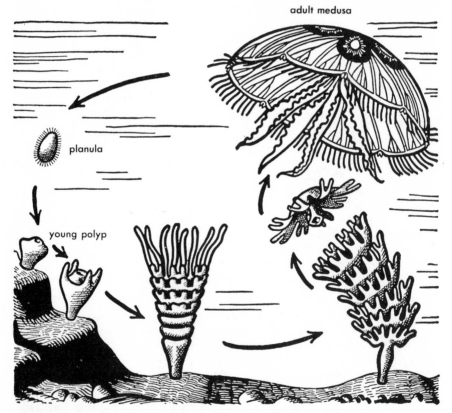

Fig. 2-9. Life cycle of *Aurelia.* (Reprinted from Buchsbaum, *Animals Without Backbones,* 1948. Courtesy of The University of Chicago Press.)

the distal end of the polyp in the same way as slices might be removed from an ever-growing loaf of bread. The medusae swim away, grow, acquire gonads, and eventually reproduce sexually.

This is an exceptional type of life cycle. There are some things about it of interest in connection with what was said previously. First of all, there are *two* stages capable of dispersal: the planula and the medusa. Second, we are again dealing with an organism in which fertilization is left largely to chance, and in which asexual reproduction provides a compensatory safeguard. But the question of immediate concern to us here is which stage of the life cycle ought to be called the adult. Is it the polyp or the medusa? If we were to restrict our definition, so that an adult is to be viewed not merely as a stage that reproduces, but one that reproduces *sexually,* then of course the adult would become the medusa. This might be particularly appropriate if it could be proven that the medusa is evolutionarily the older stage and that the polyp was only acquired secondarily and represented in essence an asexually reproducing larva. But the question of which came first, the polyp or the medusa, is by no means settled. It is quite possible that both stages are of equal evolutionary age, and it is even argued sometimes that the polyp may be the older one. At any rate, there are coelenterates in the world today, such as *Hydra,* which develop one polyp generation after another without intervening medusae (just as there are species of jellyfish that skip the polyp stage). How does our definition of adult apply, for instance, to *Hydra?* Are we to say that *Hydra* is an adult *only* when it develops testes and ovaries, and that it reverts to immaturity whenever it reproduces asexually by budding? Does this mean that *Amoeba* never reaches adulthood? Or should we return to our original definition and let an adult be *any* stage that reproduces? But would this not mean that *Aurelia* has *two* adults: the polyp and the medusa?

One might also consider the following case. Salamanders, like frogs, have an aquatic larva that breathes with gills, and a terrestrial adult in which the gills are lost and are replaced by lungs. However, it sometimes happens that salamanders achieve reproductive maturity before the gills are lost. Textbooks of biology often describe this phenomenon as illustrating reproduction in the larval stage, and call it *neoteny.* The implication here seems to be that the criterion for adulthood in salamanders is not so much the maturation of the gonads but the loss of gills.

We have gotten ourselves bogged down in a semantic argument. "Adulthood" is evidently not an easy thing to define. In biology, perhaps more than in many fields, it is easy to get oneself frustratingly involved in semantics. The extraordinary adaptive diversity by which a biological phenomenon so frequently manifests itself can make it rather difficult to characterize the phenomenon by a clear-cut all-encompassing definition. But however frustrating the attempted formulation of an appropriate definition may be, it seldom involves wasted effort. One is forced to seek example after example, comparing and contrasting them as one goes along, and in so doing one is often led to interesting discoveries and generalizations of which one might hitherto have been unaware.

Sometimes it seems justifiable to advance a definition merely for the purpose of a specific argument. We have used such *operational* definitions ourselves in our earlier discussion. We applied the term "leisure time," for example, because we felt it would simplify our discussion of continuous and discontinuous feeding habits. We used the term for lack of a better one, and we would not like to see it generally adopted simply because we feel that the term itself is not a particularly good one (especially because "leisure" implies time in which to "loll around and do nothing," which is exactly what organisms do *not* do in their leisure time). But since at the outset of our argument we defined precisely what we meant by leisure time, we felt that its use would not be dangerously misleading. If one thinks for a moment about biological terms of wide usage, one realizes that many of them are very difficult and sometimes impossible to define with absolute precision. This does not detract from the fact that such terms are nevertheless useful. Think of the term "life," and try to define it. Or, try to define "death."

It is only fitting that we should give some consideration to "death" at the end of our discussion of the adult. In a human being we associate the onset of death with the cessation of the heartbeat. The criterion seems appropriate, since with the stopping of the heart all muscular activity comes to a prompt halt. This is because the nervous system, which ordinarily activates muscles, is highly sensitive to oxygen deprivation, and it ceases to function the moment blood flow stops. However, for minutes or even hours after "death" certain cells from the body continue to live. They could probably be excised and shown to be capable of growth in tissue culture. Evidently, the death of the organism does not coincide with the death of each of its cellular components. Again we find ourselves confronted with a troublesome matter of definition.

From a philosophical standpoint there is something ominous about death. But there is also something adaptively significant about it, which, as biologists, we cannot ignore. Why is it that among the millions of organisms in the world today, both plant and animal, not a single one seems to have departed from the norm and achieved an unlimited lifespan? One could of course argue that such species *do* exist, but that ordinarily their potentially unlimited life is brought to an untimely end through accident, predation, or disease. If, on the other hand, they do *not* exist, is it because there might be a universal selective disadvantage to immortality? We would here again have to define precisely what we mean by immortality. Could an individual hydra that has the potential for reproducing asexually in its exact genetic image for unending generations be considered potentially immortal?

MAINTENANCE OF THE INTERNAL MILIEU

Under the broad category of maintenance we shall examine the processes of respiration, circulation, excretion, and osmoregulation. Thus far we have dealt primarily with behavioral adaptations related to growth and reproduction, and with structural adaptations associated with nutrition and development. Our emphasis now will be on the physiological aspects of adaptation.

Respiration and Circulation

Molecular oxygen, which constitutes about 20 percent of the atmosphere, and which in lesser amounts is found dissolved in all the oceans and inland waters of the world, is a most general requisite of life. The need for oxygen is, in fact, a basic property that both animals and plants have in common. The need is *not* universal, for there are organisms (or parts of organisms) that can survive indefinitely or for limited times in the complete absence of oxygen. But although such organisms are important in their own right, they are definitely the exception.

Thanks mostly to the advances of modern biochemistry, the role of oxygen in cellular metabolism is properly understood. Oxygen is essential for the process of *cellular respiration*.

The formation and maintenance of a living system requires continuous expenditure of energy. The ultimate source of the energy expended by *all* organisms is sunlight, but sunlight as such cannot be exploited by the living machinery. It must first be transformed into chemical energy. This transformation is what green plants accomplish when, in the process of photosynthesis, they "lock" the radiant energy of sunlight into the glucose molecule. Cellular respiration is the process whereby glucose is broken down and its contained energy made available to power the cell's machinery. Plants can rely on glucose that they themselves make in photosynthesis. Animals, on the other hand, must have prefabricated organic fuel, and this is why they must feed on plants, or on animals that in turn feed on plants. Cellular respiration can be expressed by the following general formula:

$$C_6H_{12}O_6 + 6O_2 \longrightarrow 6CO_2 + 6H_2O + 686{,}000 \text{ Calories}$$

(1 mole)   of energy

The energy liberated is not released as heat energy in a single burst, or cells might literally incinerate themselves. The degradation of glucose to carbon dioxide and water occurs piecemeal through a series of chemical reactions, each of which requires special enzymes. The energy of the original glucose molecule is thus released in small "packets" along the way, and instead of being entirely dissipated as heat, it is trapped, so to speak, in the form of high-energy bonds within certain molecules that serve specifically for energy storage. Whenever the living system performs work of any kind, it is drawing upon the high-energy reserve stored in these molecules. The above equation is thus a simplified representation of a highly complex biochemical process that actually involves a lengthy series of individual chemical steps.

When we think of an animal performing work, we usually think of work accomplished through muscular activity. In active animals such as ourselves, most energy is indeed invested in muscular work. But there are many other types of work that a living system performs. The synthesis of molecules, the conduction of nerve impulses, secretory and absorptive processes—these and many others all involve the expenditure of energy. There is not a moment in the life of an organism when it is not performing some kinds of biological work.

When we examine the above formula for respiration, several things become apparent beyond the primary fact that oxygen is a requisite for completion of the process. There are two end products of respiration, carbon dioxide and water. Water is the major constituent of living matter, and its formation in respiration is of no consequence. It may even be a distinct asset for organisms living on land where water is at a premium. Carbon dioxide, by contrast, yields a toxic acid (carbonic acid) when dissolved in water, and its accumulation cannot be tolerated. For a respiring organism it is as essential to eliminate carbon dioxide as it is to obtain oxygen.

Both carbon dioxide and oxygen are relatively small molecules and they can diffuse readily across cell membranes. But—and this is an important *but*—the membranes must be moist. Hence, in order for a proper respiratory exchange to be assured, an organism is forced to maintain some portion of its body surface in a moist and permeable condition. This is an adaptive necessity that not a *single* organism has been able to circumvent. A moist, permeable membrane is the primary common feature of lungs, gills, and any other respiratory organs.

With these basic facts as a foundation, and bearing in mind what was said earlier about the insect tracheal system, let us now examine a few respiratory systems of animals and see what particular adaptive significance there might be to the unique refinements of each.

The first thing that a general survey of animals would reveal is that some of them have no special respiratory devices at all. Virtually all of these are aquatic, and most of them are small. Protozoans belong to this category. These animals simply breathe through their entire body surface. The surface is moist, and is sufficiently large relative to the bulk of the enclosed cell, so there is no "need" for gills or other respiratory structures. The fact that these animals are small is important. The laws of diffusion tell us that oxygen and carbon dioxide molecules could only move through the aqueous milieu of a cell at a very slow rate at best. This is obviously of no serious consequence to a tiny protozoan in which oxygen and carbon dioxide molecules never have very far to go in their movement to and from the cell membrane.

There are also some larger organisms that lack special respiratory organs and that breathe through their entire body surface. Flatworms, including such familiar forms as planarians, flukes, and tapeworms, are of this kind. Living in a watery medium enables them to maintain a moist permeable body covering. Also, as indicated by their very name, they are flat, which means that no cell in their system is very far removed from the body surface. The slowness of diffusion, therefore, poses no serious problems for a flatworm, because the distances over which the respiratory gases must diffuse inside the animal are never very large. There are some flatworms in the tropics that live on land. They too respire through the body surface. But they live confined to cramped humid quarters, such as under logs or in decaying leaf litter, where the water loss that inevitably occurs through their moist integument is held to a minimum.

There are two major circumstances under which simple mechanisms of respiration such as those of protozoans and flatworms can no longer satisfy the demands of an animal. Such systems are inadequate for bulky animals and for animals leading a truly exposed terrestrial existence.

The bulkier the animal, the greater are the internal distances over which the respiratory gases must be conveyed, and if this conveyance is to take place in any way efficiently, it must be by a means other than simple diffusion. Such a means may of course be provided by a circulatory system, which ensures that distribution is by the free flow of blood coursing through a more or less extensive network of internal vessels. We need only think of our own circulatory system to realize the tremendous levels of complexity that such systems may achieve.

The blood of animals is not always colorless. Many contain so-called respiratory pigments that vastly improve the oxygen-carrying capacity of blood. Two common pigment types that occur in animals are hemoglobin and hemocyanin. The first, hemoglobin, is red in color and is the pigment that gives the characteristic color to our own and other mammalian blood. It is found also in birds, reptiles, amphibians, fish, annelids, and certain mollusks (there is even hemoglobin in some plants, but there is a very special story associated with this). Hemocyanin, on the other hand, is blue in color, and is the characteristic blood pigment of some mollusks, and certain non-insect arthropods. Both these pigments, in order to function in respiration, must have certain properties in common. They must be able to combine loosely with oxygen in order to ensure that they will release oxygen readily when the tissues demand it. In other words, they must be constructed in such a way that they have an affinity for oxygen in areas of high oxygen tension (at the lungs, or gills) and release oxygen in areas of low oxygen tension (the oxygen-consuming tissues). Both of these pigments possess this capacity, but their relative efficiencies as oxygen carriers differ.

The most efficient types of blood yet evolved are those containing hemoglobin. For example, 25 times more oxygen is contained in a cubic centimeter of mammalian blood than in a similar amount of sea water. Moreover, mammalian blood can hold at least three times more oxygen than the blood of an animal that has hemocyanin instead of hemoglobin.

The adaptive significance of blood pigments cannot be overemphasized. The tremendous respiratory demands of animals such as vertebrates, which lead a highly active life, could not have been met satisfactorily with a pigment-free blood.

It is interesting in this connection to examine a relatively large animal—a starfish—that lacks blood pigments and does not even possess what one could truly call a circulatory system. Inside the starfish (Fig. 2–10) is a large body space, or coelom, which surrounds all of the internal organs. The coelom is filled with a liquid that is very similar to sea water and contains no respiratory pigment. In fact, individual organs may be removed from a starfish and placed in plain sea water, where they will live for hours or even days.

The starfish's external surface is covered with an epidermis underlain by bony plates, or ossicles. Spaces exist between the ossicles, and through these spaces project thin fingerlike diverticuli that are in direct contact with the coelom (see *skin gills,* in Fig. 2–10). Thus, oxygen diffusing from the sea water through the diverticuli passes directly into the coelomic fluid. In a starfish there is no heart or other device for stirring the coelomic fluid. Yet the fluid is not altogether stagnant. The lining of the coelom is beset with cilia, which through constant lashing action impart a slight but nevertheless significant motion to the fluid within.

Starfish are by no means at the verge of extinction. They are surviving effectively, and have been doing so for millions of years, despite their evidently highly rudimentary respiratory and circulatory adaptations. But they are restricted to a most sluggish way of life. Normally they move about slowly with their hundreds of tube feet over the ocean floor in search of a molluscan dinner. There is no reason to suppose that they will not be leading a similar existence several million years hence. But there is also no reason to suppose that with their present anatomical equipment they will give rise, in the near evolutionary future, to some fast-swimming pelagic forms or terrestrial forms.

Not all active animals have blood pigments. Insects, for example, do not. But this is not unexpected, since in insects the tracheae convey air directly to the cells, and the circulatory system plays no mediating role in the conveyance of respiratory gases. Again, however, there are exceptions. Hemoglobin is known to occur in certain fly larvae. One of these, *Gastrophilus,* is

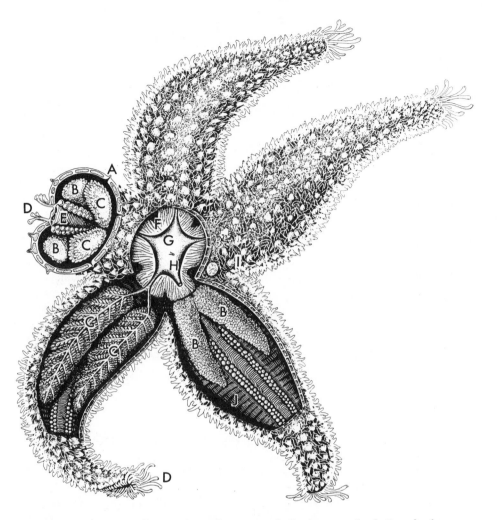

Fig. 2-10. Starfish anatomy. A: skin gills; B: gonad; C: digestive gland; D: tube feet (stalks); E: tube feet (sacs); F: stomach (eversible region); G: stomach (fixed region), H: anus; I: madreporite; J: body cavity. (Courtesy of Natural History Magazine.)

a parasitic larva living in the stomach of horses. Its hemoglobin is not in the blood, but in cells associated with the tracheolar ends. The adaptive significance of the hemoglobin of this larva becomes evident when one considers that the oxygen tension in its habitat is at times very low.

It would also be incorrect to say that *only* very active animals have blood pigments. The role of blood pigments in a highly inactive animal may be a very special one. A good example is provided by *Arenicola,* the lugworm (Fig. 3–11). This marine annelid spends most of its time in a tube that it builds in sand. For the site of its burrow it usually selects a spot just above the low-tide mark. This means that when the tide has receded the animal finds itself trapped in a tube containing but a residue of sea water from which the oxygen is rapidly depleted. Its survival under these conditions is aided by the fact that its blood contains hemoglobin. At high tide, an excess of oxygen is available because fresh sea water is continuously circulating through the burrow. During this period the animal actually does not need its hemoglobin, and it can function perfectly well by using oxygen dissolved in the blood. But the hemoglobin nevertheless becomes loaded with oxygen, and it is from this "load" that the animal subsists later at low tide, when conditions once again become critical.

Intimately associated with the evolution of circulatory systems is that of special respiratory organs. Think of a rat, bird, turtle, fish, frog, lobster, or squid. All of these have elaborate circulatory systems, complete with blood pigments and special pumps in the form of hearts, and all of them also have either gills or lungs. This means that the animal confines its respiratory exchange to a specialized and restricted portion of its body. Such organs become *most* effective when they are linked with a circulatory system that ferries the respiratory gases between the exchange surfaces and the remaining tissues of the animal. Insects, because of the peculiar nature of the tracheal system, are again exceptional.

Gills and lungs are essentially highly folded respiratory membranes. In the case of a gill, the membrane is an *outfolding* of the integument; in a lung, it is an *infolding*. Gills are the predominant respiratory organs of aquatic animals, and they are found in a great diversity of forms, including many mollusks, polychaete annelids, crustaceans, fish, larval amphibians, and others. Their susceptibility to desiccation renders a gill unsuitable for life on land (although there are some animals, including the very interesting crustaceans called sow bugs, which retain gills despite their terrestrial existence). In a lung, the epithelium is not as exposed to desiccation because it is confined within a sac inside the body of the animal. All terrestrial vertebrates have lungs, and there are lunglike organs in some terrestrial snails. Despite the sheltered condition of the respiratory epithelium in a lung, the amount of water that is nevertheless unavoidably lost through breathing is by no means negligible. The condensation of water droplets on a window "fogged" by breath gives some indication of the magnitude of water loss involved.

It is easy to underestimate the enormity of the respiratory surface available for gas exchange in a lung or gill (Figs. 2–11, 3–8). The total area of our own pulmonary epithelium undoubtedly exceeds several times that of our entire body surface. As an interesting exercise, the reader may attempt

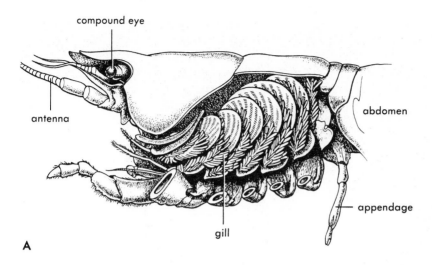

A

B

Fig. 2-11. A: Gills of a crayfish. These are ordinarily hidden under the
carapace, which has been dissected away. B: Enlarged view of a small portion
of a gill, showing the respiratory filaments. They are hollow, and blood courses
through them. Each gill is beset with hundreds of such filaments. (A, from
Griffin, *Animal Structure and Function*, Holt, Rinehart and Winston, Inc.)

Fig. 2-12. Gills, a, of a fish, exposed by removal of the operculum.

to estimate the magnitude of the respiratory gill epithelium of a fish (Fig. 2–12). The anatomy of the gill can be easily worked out with a hand lens or stereomicroscope, and a few simple measurements and calculations should lead to a reasonable first-approximation value. The results are unbelievable at first, and they should certainly dispel any feeling one might have that the restriction of gas exchange to special respiratory organs results in an undue reduction of the respiratory surface. One wonders how large an area might be provided by the collective total of respiratory exchange surfaces in the tracheolar endings of an insect such as *Aedes*.

We shall now examine one more animal in detail, not so much because it is an unusually interesting one in many respects, but because it illustrates a special point. It is an example of an animal that has departed radically from the mode of life of its near ancestors, and it is quite evident that this departure is very largely attributable to special adaptive refinements of the circulatory and respiratory systems. The animal is a cephalopod mollusk, the common squid, *Loligo* (Fig. 2–13).

Anyone who has observed a squid locomote is impressed with its great speed. This in itself is rather unmolluscan. Mollusks other than cephalopods, and including such diverse forms as clams, oysters, slugs, snails, and chitons, are sluggish at best, and often sedentary. The squid must evidently have vastly more efficient respiratory and circulatory systems than those of its non-cephalopod relatives. This is indeed the case.

Most mollusks have an open circulatory system not altogether unlike that of *Aedes;* that is, blood flows from the major vessels directly into body spaces rather than into capillaries. In the squid there are capillary networks present, and there is therefore a continuous and directional flow of blood through a vessel system, without any intervening spaces or "pools" susceptible to temporary stagnation.

The respiratory system of the squid is also especially well developed. Large gills, densely irrigated by capillaries, lie inside the mantle cavity. Fresh oxygenated sea water is constantly available to the gills, since the animal is continually pumping water in and out of the mantle cavity during the normal course of locomation. *Loligo* swims by jet propulsion, with thrust provided by the expulsion of water during the exhalant phase of the pumping cycle.

The presence of narrow-gauge capillaries, and particularly their dense networks in the gills, imposes a formidable extra demand on the pumping power of the heart. A squid has, in fact, *three* hearts. In addition to the

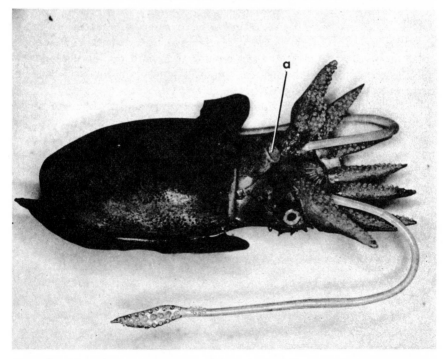

Fig. 2-13. A squid (*Sepia officinalis*). This is a relative of the *Loligo* mentioned in the text; a, excurrent funnel through which jets of water are expelled during locomotion. (Photograph of glass model.)

single one usual for mollusks, it has two extra ones associated with the gills, serving specifically to force blood through the gill capillaries. A squid also has a particularly high concentration of hemocyanin in its blood. It is impossible to imagine how this type of animal could have evolved from a bottom-dwelling ancestor and take up an active pelagic existence if all these and many other adaptive changes had not occurred.

At the outset of our discussion on respiration we mentioned that there are certain organisms that can withstand temporary or even indefinite periods of oxygen deprivation. In such organisms there takes place what is known as *anaerobic* respiration. In the absence of oxygen, it is impossible for the glucose molecule to be degraded in its entirety to carbon dioxide and water. The molecule is only partially broken down, and the end products are different. In yeast, alcohol is formed (anaerobic respiration in yeasts is called fermentation), and in animals the product is lactic acid. The notable thing about anaerobic respiration is that it results in only a partial liberation of the energy stored in glucose. In aerobic respiration, where the degradation of the glucose molecule is complete, 686,000 calories per mole of glucose are made available. In anaerobic respiration, where the degradation is partial, only 40,000 calories are liberated.

The adaptive significance of anaerobic respiration is that it enables an organism, or a part of an organism, to obtain at least *some* energy from glucose during periods of total oxygen lack. Our muscles, for instance, can operate temporarily under such conditions. The resulting inevitable accumulation of lactic acid eventually leads to "cramps."

Animals capable of withstanding anaerobic conditions for long periods of time have open to them for colonization environments that would otherwise be totally uninhabitable. Such environments are sometimes highly propitious in other respects. Inside the gut of vertebrates and other animals the oxygen tension may be vanishingly small. Compensating for this is the vast amount of food available and the relative freedom from competition. Intestinal worms probably respire anaerobically much of the time. Since they lead relatively inactive lives, their energy demands are relatively low.

Excretion of Nitrogenous Wastes

We mentioned in the first chapter that all animals are faced with the necessity of eliminating waste materials that contain nitrogen. These nitrogenous wastes are the inevitable end products of the metabolic degradation of proteins. Proteins are the principal nitrogen-containing compounds in a living system, and the nitrogen atoms in the nitrogenous wastes stem largely from the amino-nitrogen of the amino acids that make up proteins. We have seen how the adult *Aedes*, and other insects that are adapted to a terrestrial existence, excrete a solid nitrogenous waste to conserve their water supply.

Let us now examine this whole matter of the elimination of nitrogenous wastes from a broader point of view.

Judging from the diversity with which so many biological adaptations manifest themselves, one might have thought that nature employs a host of nitrogen-containing molecules as a vehicle for nitrogen excretion. This is not the case. In fact, with some exceptions, only three principal molecules are employed by animals for this purpose; ammonia, urea, and uric acid. Their structural formulas are shown in Fig. 2–14. Note the nitrogen atoms in each.

Whether an animal excretes one or the other of these molecules is not determined so much by the particular taxonomic group to which it belongs as by the environment in which it lives. We shall now examine in some detail what we mean by this. It should be mentioned at the outset, however, that an animal does not necessarily produce only one of these compounds. Most species excrete more than one, but usually a single one predominates, often by far. So, for instance, when we say that man excretes urea, we really mean that this is the *principal* nitrogenous waste in his urine. He also excretes uric acid and ammonia in lesser amounts.

Ammonia is a common excretory product, but it is also a very toxic one, much more so than either uric acid or urea. A survey of ammonia-excreting animals reveals that these forms are aquatic. Since ammonia is readily soluble in water, it can be eliminated by diffusion, or by actively forcing a dilute solution of it out of the system. Since ammonia is toxic in very low concentrations (it kills a rabbit at 5 milligrams per 100 milliliters of blood), it follows that the amount of water required by the organism to "wash out" the ammonia is accordingly great. This is why ammonia excretion is impractical for terrestrial animals or any others living under conditions where water is scarce. If man were to excrete ammonia instead of urea, his daily urine output—as well as his compensatory water intake—would rise many fold.

The size of the organism bears some relation to the particular mechanism employed in ammonia elimination. In minute animals such as protozoans, ammonia is passed to the outside simply by diffusion. The same holds for sponges and coelenterates. In flatworms, a good deal of ammonia is undoubtedly eliminated, like carbon dioxide, by diffusion through the body

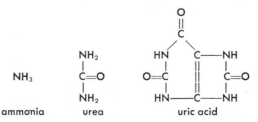

Fig. 2-14. Structural formulas of three common nitrogenous excretory products.

wall. But flatworms are endowed with certain specialized cells that serve specifically for the forcible expulsion of excess water from their systems, and this water can evidently serve as an additional route for ammonia elimination. These special cells, or flame cells, are constructed in a unique way (Fig. 2–15). Each has a canal running the length of it. One end of the canal ends blindly, and the other leads to a collecting system of canals that eventually converge at an excretory pore. At the blind end, a small tuft of cilia beats constantly, forcing a stream of water down the canal. This beating resembles the burning of a candle flame and gives the cell its name. Through this mechanism, water—plus presumably dissolved ammonia—is quickly and efficiently flushed from the animal. In many fresh water protozoans there are contractile vacuoles present that similarly serve for water elimination, and that might therefore also be expected to serve—perhaps only incidentally—for ammonia elimination.

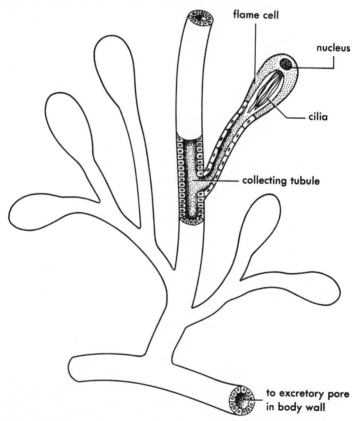

flame cell

nucleus

cilia

collecting tubule

to excretory pore
in body wall

Fig. 2-15. Portion of excretory system of a flatworm with flame cells. (From Griffin, *Animal Structure and Function,* Holt, Rinehart and Winston, Inc.)

In annelid worms there are already fairly elaborate "kidneys" present. These will be described in some detail in Chapter 3. It will suffice to say here that a single worm may contain dozens of such kidneys, or *nephridia,* each consisting of a more or less convoluted tube, opening by one end into the body cavity, and by the other directly to the outside. Annelids are a predominantly aquatic group, and their excretory product is ammonia. Despite the presence of these special nephridia, aquatic annelids probably still lose much of their ammonia by simple diffusion through the integument. Most animals with a wet and permeable body wall probably eliminate some of their ammonia this way. But the larger the bulk of the animal, the greater becomes its dependence on special organs for excretion.

Before shifting our attention from ammonia to other nitrogenous wastes, we may again examine the starfish (Fig. 2–10) as an example of an animal that, despite its bulk, can perform, without special organs, functions that in other animals of comparable size usually require them. The starfish, it may be recalled, lacks specific respiratory and circulatory organs. It also lacks special organs of excretion. It eliminates ammonia, in the same manner as carbon dioxide, through the thin and permeable fingerlike diverticuli that projects between the ossicles of its body wall. Such a seemingly "inefficient" system might not be adequate for a more active animal with higher metabolism, but it evidently does well for a starfish.

Organisms living in a habitat in which water may be at a premium do not excrete ammonia, but instead produce urea or uric acid. We may begin by examining an amphibian such as a frog, which divides its life between the aquatic and terrestrial environment.

The egg and tadpole live in fresh water, and for them there is essentially no critical need for water conservation. As one might expect, both stages produce ammonia. For the adult frog, however, which is already susceptible to desiccation by virtue of its moist and permeable skin, survival on land presupposes that water be conserved. By excreting urea, the frog is capable of producing a much less copious urine than if it had to drain ammonia from its system. The tolerance for urea is much higher than that for ammonia. Urea is commonly present at levels exceeding 30 mg per 100 ml of blood, and amounts well in excess of this may often be withstood. This is why considerably fewer molecules of water are needed to flush out a molecule of urea from a living system than are needed per molecule of ammonia.

Uric acid is an especially advantageous type of nitrogenous waste to be produced by a land dweller because it can be eliminated with virtually no water loss. The ability to produce uric acid has evolved more than once among animals. Besides insects, both reptiles and birds produce it, and it is also known to occur in certain land snails.

There are some remarkable parallels between the excretory mechanisms of birds and reptiles on the one hand, and insects on the other. It will be recalled that the Malpighian tubules (Fig. 1–6) do not open to the outside by orifices of their own, but connect to the terminal portion of the digestive tract. In insects and other terrestrial animals this last part of the gut functions in water reabsorption, which enables the animals to retrieve a maximum of water from the feces before their elimination. Since the Malpighian tubules are of narrow gauge, they could easily get clogged with uric acid crystals unless these are ferried along as a semisolid paste with a certain amount of water. If the tubules were to open directly to the outside, this water would be lost. But by having them open into the hind-gut, the water can be reabsorbed, and the crystals can then be forcibly defecated as part of the dry or almost dry fecal pellet. In many insects, and particularly in those living in desert or other dry conditions, the water extraction from the fecal pellet is nearly complete. "Urination" in such insects involves hardly any water loss at all.

In reptiles and birds the ducts draining the kidneys do not lead out on their own as they do, for instance, in mammals. These ducts share with the digestive tract a common efferent conduit that leads to the anus. The adaptive significance of this arrangement as regards water conservation may well be the same as in insects, although the extent to which water is reabsorbed in the common conduit remains to be demonstrated. There can be no question, however, that the water loss accompanying the elimination of uric acid can—under those environmental circumstances that demand it— be held to a minimum. The desert-dwelling horned toad *Phrynosoma* (which is not a toad at all, but a lizard) puts out a solid ball of uric acid crystals. The droppings of birds offer clear evidence that defecation and urination occur together in these animals. The dark material in the droppings is fecal matter, and the white material is uric acid.

There are other similarities between insects, birds, and reptiles. All lay shelled (so-called *cleidoic*) eggs. In a real sense such a shelled egg represents a closed system. Except for the exchange of respiratory gases, there is nothing that leaves or enters the egg during its entire life. Food in the form of yolk is provided beforehand by the mother, and metabolic wastes remain captive within the egg until hatching. If such a closed system is examined in the light of the special adaptive demands it places on excretion, it is clear that neither ammonia nor urea could be the nitrogenous waste of the embryo. Imagine the disastrous consequences if ammonia were produced. Unable to diffuse outward at an appropriately high rate, it would soon build up to a toxic level and the bird would never see the light of day. Urea can be tolerated at higher concentrations, but the accumulation of this molecule would begin causing difficulties even before toxic concentrations were actually achieved. Urea is a relatively small molecule, highly soluble in water. Its accumulation within the embryo—either inside its cells, or in intracellular spaces—would eventually result in an intolerable impairment of the required osmotic balance. The embryo has no alternatives other than to shut off its protein metabolism altogether, or to produce an insoluble and hence osmotically inactive nitrogenous waste. The former alternative is clearly no solution at all. For the latter alternative, uric acid is an acceptable candidate, and it is indeed the one of choice. Birds and reptiles possess a sac, called the *allantois,* which projects ventrally from the embryo, and into which uric acid crystals are dumped during development. At the time of hatching, the sac and its contents are discarded.

In insects, the cleidoic egg is also to be regarded as the developmental stage that could not have been achieved without the embryo's ability to produce an insoluble nitrogenous waste. And we can say the same thing for the pupa, which is after all a similarly closed system. Thus, the ability to produce uric acid can, in a sense, be viewed as a "preadaptation" without which complete metamorphosis as we know it in insects could never have evolved.

We have already seen that an animal may not necessarily excrete the same nitrogenous waste at all stages of its development. The tadpole excretes primarily ammonia, and the adult frog produces mainly urea. There is a good deal of evidence to indicate that reptiles evolved from amphibians, and that subsequently birds and mammals were derived from the reptiles. It is conceivable that during the early evolutionary transition from amphibian to reptile, one of the first major changes to occur was the shift from an aquatic amphibian egg to a terrestrial cleidoic egg. The change from the typical semiterrestrial *adult* amphibian with moist skin, to the truly terrestrial reptile with dry impermeable skin, might only have taken place later. In other words, uric acid excretion might have begun as an adaptation to life within the cleidoic egg, and was only later adopted by the adult.

The aquatic larva of *Aedes* excretes uric acid like its terrestrial parent. We might take this to be evidence in favor of the "irrevocability" of evolution; that is, once insects and their terrestrial larvae evolved the mechanism for uric acid excretion, there was no departure from this mechanism in those larvae that secondarily adopted an aquatic existence. One might have predicted that a shift to fresh water would be accompanied by a "return" to ammonia excretion, but such a prediction is obviously contradicted by *Aedes.* However, there are certain aquatic insect larvae that, like that of *Aedes,* are descendants of terrestrial forms, but that *do* excrete substantial amounts of ammonia.

Before leaving the subject of excretion, it should be pointed out that many land dwellers excrete urea and not uric acid. Mammals are in that class. They excrete urea, unavoidably dissolved in copious amounts of water. During development, a young mammal need not employ a different system of excretion. This is because very close contact is established in the placenta between the blood supply of the mother and embryo; waste materials from the embryo diffuse directly into the blood of the mother and then are conveyed to her kidneys for excretion.

This book deals exclusively with animal adaptations and we have therefore avoided discussing plants, although it must be evident to the reader that many of the general statements made about adaptations apply to plants as well as animals. As regards excretion there is something peculiar worth noting about plants. Metabolic degradation of proteins is not at all restricted to animals, but occurs in all living systems. Plants, too, must therefore have a way of coping with the amino-nitrogen from degraded proteins. Why, then, is it that plants do not, so to speak, urinate?

Osmoregulation

When we discussed osmoregulation in *Aedes* we stressed that it is necessary for an organism to preserve at all times a proper osmotic milieu in its tissues and tissue fluids. In other words, it must maintain within itself an over-all constancy in the concentration of water and that of the solutes dissolved in it. This may be a more or less demanding effort depending on how great the osmotic discrepancy is between the organism and its environment. Moreover, it may be a varying effort, since the magnitude of the discrepancy fluctuates with changes of environment.

We have seen specific adaptations by which osmotic conditions are regulated in the *Aedes* larva. The animal possesses an impermeable cuticle, anal gills capable of selectively absorbing salts from the external medium, and Malpighian tubules that can remove ions from the blood. There is enormous variation in the osmoregulatory ability of different animals, and the adaptations that serve specifically for enforcement of the osmotic balance are many and diverse.

To begin, let us focus on some generalizations. The vast majority of primitive marine animals—that is, animals that never left the oceanic environment in which they evolved—are at virtual osmotic equilibrium with the water around them. Their inner osmotic conditions are essentially those of sea water itself, and they therefore have no need to guard constantly against gain or loss of water and salts. Fresh-water animals, on the other hand, are surrounded by a medium disproportionately rich in water and poor in salts. Such animals must "hold on" to the salts, while at the same time preventing their tissues from becoming flooded with excess water. For terrestrial animals the shortage of salts does not pose nearly as great a problem as the threat of desiccation. We have already seen how some of them are adapted to minimize water loss.

These three categories of animals—marine, fresh-water, and terrestrial—are the main types to consider when dealing with osmoregulation. But one of them, the marine, includes a most interesting subcategory, made up of those animals that have secondarily invaded the oceans. These animals, by virtue of their terrestrial or fresh-water ancestry, have inherited an internal osmotic concentration below that of sea water, and they preserved this reduced concentration when they went to sea. Thus, they find themselves "at odds" with their environment. For such secondarily marine animals, the sea is a desiccating and excessively salty environment. These animals include important groups. In addition to such forms as seals and whales, which are derived from terrestrial mammals, there are the marine fish, whose immediate ancestors came from fresh water. As unreasonable as it might seem, a marine fish is, in a sense, a continually "thirsty" animal. Let us now examine specific examples in some detail.

Marine invertebrates, as mentioned, are at virtual equilibrium with their environment. Life is presumed to have arisen in the ocean, and the osmotic similarity between sea water and the tissue fluids of primitive marine organisms is often cited as supporting evidence to that effect. The assumption seems to be that for the first organisms it was adaptively advantageous to have their internal milieu mimic that of the surrounding medium. This may well be true, but it would be erroneous to think that the tissue fluid of these animals is similar to sea water in all respects. Whereas they do contain salts and water in about the same *total* proportions as sea water, and hence are in fact in equilibrium with the surrounding medium, they do not contain salts in the same *relative* proportions as they are in the sea. For instance, tissue fluid commonly contains more potassium and less magnesium than sea water. These organisms must therefore continually regulate their ionic concentration to maintain the discrepancy.

Many marine invertebrates can operate their osmoregulatory mechanisms only as long as they are in full-strength sea water. Brackish water, such as prevails in estuaries, kills them. But there are others that do live in estuaries and that evidently can cope with wide ionic fluctuations. We shall not dwell on these except to point out that such forms are of particular interest because they offer clues to the types of osmoregulatory mechanisms that must have prevailed in ancestors of fresh-water and terrestrial forms while they were making their transition from the oceans.

The echinoderms are an example of a group that can only withstand undiluted sea water. If a starfish is transferred to fresh water, it quickly stops moving and dies in minutes. Water diffuses into the animal, and there is no mechanism for flushing it back out again at an adequately fast rate. Among the annelids, crustaceans, and mollusks, there *are* estuarine forms, and all of these groups also include forms that have permanently moved into fresh water. Echinoderms do not include a single fresh-water form. In a way this may seem surprising, since the fresh-water habitat fulfills some of the requisites that would seem basic for echinoderm survival. There are many mollusks in fresh water, and a starfish could presumably survive on them without departing from its ancestral diet. Other echinoderms, which are scavengers, would have found an abundance of sediment on which to feed. Currents should not have posed problems for adult echinoderms that move with hundreds of tenaciously adhering tube feet. However, currents would have caused difficulties for the planktonic larvae, and the early developmental stages would indeed have required modification. This in itself might have been a major obstacle, which, coupled with the need for adapting to adverse osmotic conditions, made the transition to fresh water insurmountably difficult.

In fresh water, animals must conserve salts and eliminate, or prevent the influx of, excess water. This is accomplished in diverse ways. Many Protozoans employ contractile vacuoles to "bail out" the surplus water that constantly enters them by diffusion (Fig. 2–16). The elaborate canal system that drains the flame cells of flatworms may similarly serve for water evacuation.

Fresh-water fish have been studied in some detail. These animals minimize the amount of water that is swallowed (just as does the *Aedes* larva), and relatively little water penetrates through their skin. But there is a constant high influx of water through the permeable respiratory surfaces of the gills, which, if allowed to build up, would kill the animal. The kidneys filter this excess water from the blood and eliminate it via the urine. A high urinary output is thus obligatory for a fresh-water fish, but it is not to be viewed strictly as a "necessary evil," since a copious urine also provides a ready vehicle for ammonia elimination. The fish can withhold salts to some

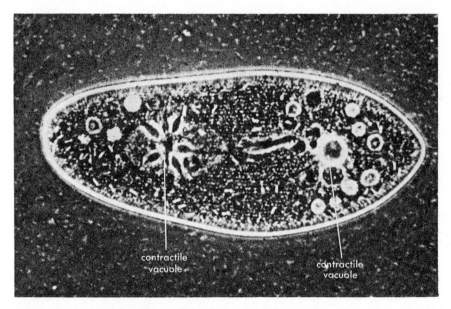

Fig. 2-16. *Paramecium caudatum,* showing contractile vacuoles. (From Boolootian and Heyneman, *An Illustrated Laboratory Text in Zoology,* Holt, Rinehart and Winston, Inc.)

extent from the urine, but some are nevertheless lost. The deficit that would eventually ensue is prevented by a compensatory salt absorption through the gills. The osmoregulatory mechanism of fresh-water fish is thus seen to bear some remarkable similarities to that of the *Aedes* larva, although of course the organs involved are totally different.

The case of a marine fish is an especially interesting one. Unlike its fresh-water counterpart, this animal must deal with a shortage of water and an excess of salt. It constantly loses water by diffusion through the gills and other permeable membranes. To make up for this, it drinks sea water continuously while urinating sparingly. The excess salt that is unavoidably absorbed with the ingested sea water is excreted through the gills. Since it urinates sparingly, one might expect a nitrogenous waste other than ammonia to be excreted. This is indeed the case. Marine fish excrete trimethylamine oxide, a molecule considerably less toxic than ammonia (although more toxic than urea), and hence one that requires correspondingly less water for its elimination.

In those fish called elasmobranchs, including sharks and their relatives, the situation is a unique one. These animals maintain a relatively high concentration of urea and trimethylamine oxide in their blood so that the net osmotic pressure within them is roughly equal to that of sea water. Thus, rather than relying, as do other marine fish, on ingestion of sea water, excretion of salts, and reduced urine production, these animals have adapted to life in the sea by bringing themselves into osmotic equilibrium with it. These animals *depend* on the high urea content in their blood. An excised shark heart can only be maintained alive and beating in the laboratory if urea is added to the medium in which it is kept. The remakable thing is that there are descendants from these marine elasmobranchs that have invaded fresh water. These animals still have urea in their blood, and hence are forced to maintain an *especially* pronounced osmotic discrepancy with the outer medium. In these elasmobranchs, urine production is even greater than it is in other fresh-water fish.

There are limits to the osmoregulatory abilities of all animals. Our own shortcomings are well illustrated by the predicament of the thirsty shipwrecked crew in a lifeboat: "Water, water every where. Nor any drop to drink." Sea water brings certain death, just as surely as prolonged unquenched thirst. We simply cannot cope with the salt. Some animals can. Marine birds, including gulls, albatross, and the like, have a special gland in the head that serves specifically for salt excretion. Such birds can and do drink sea water. Marine turtles have a comparable gland that opens in the corner of the eye.

The osmoregulatory capacities of an animal or group of animals set very definite limits upon its ecological distribution. We briefly discussed a starfish in this connection. But insects themselves are cause for thought.

Their success on land is indisputable. They also have fared well in rivers, lakes, and other inland waters. True, they have invaded fresh water mostly as larvae, but nevertheless have done so in large numbers. Why, then, is it that virtually none have become marine? There are a very few species that do live in the ocean, but unfortunately there is little known about their behavior and physiology. Considering that species of insects number well over a million, and that they are so extraordinarily diverse in their adaptive achievements, one would certainly have expected more of them to have made the move to the sea.

We do not claim to have the answer to this mystery, although we are puzzled by it nevertheless. One argument that is often advanced is that there was really no place for insects to go in the ocean since the particular marine niches available for them were already filled by another extraordinarily diverse group: the Crustacea. But crustaceans are also numerous in fresh water, and this did not keep insects out of that habitat.

Could salinity have been the reason? There are other marine animals of terrestrial ancestry that colonized the oceans despite the salinity. Some of them, such as certain seals and whales, feed largely on fish. They bypass the salt problem by taking prey that consists essentially of partially distilled sea water. But there are other marine animals that feed largely or entirely on invertebrates, and these evidently must cope with an excess of ingested salt. How they do it is not known in many cases. In the baleen whales, which feed on planktonic crustaceans, the excess salt is voided with the urine.

Our knowledge of the osmoregulatory potential of insects is scant indeed, but what little we know tells us that salinity could not in *all* cases have been the critical factor that kept them from the seas. For one thing, there are insect larvae that live in salt lakes. Also, we mentioned earlier that there are mosquito larvae that can tolerate brackish waters, and even some that can survive in full-strength or multiple-strength sea water. A clue to a possible other factor that might be barring mosquito larvae from the oceans is provided by the fact that virtually all live only in calm waters. Their breathing mechanism fails in rough waters because the siphon cannot connect with the surface. But again, there is not much we can conclude from an isolated case, for there are other insect larvae, such as those of dragonflies, mayflies, and some beetles, which are adapted to a totally submerged existence, and which nevertheless do not include marine forms.

One might reason that insects could have invaded marine water and bypassed the salt problem as some seals have done, by feeding on marine animals with body fluids of reduced salt content. Planktonic algae and crustaceans, by virtue of their small size, would have been the logical food for insects in the oceans, but the salt content of these planktonic organisms equals that of the sea. Perhaps it is asking a bit too much for insects to make the transition to sea water and to develop at the same time means for overpowering fish.

Whatever the reasons, the almost complete absence of insects from the ocean is a startling fact that deserves explanation. The obvious thing to do is to study in detail the special adaptive refinements of those few species that do live there. Only these exceptional forms can tell us "what it takes" to be a marine insect, and once we know this, the adaptive shortcomings of the remainder will become clear.

SUGGESTED READING LIST

BALDWIN, E., 1949. *An introduction to comparative biochemistry*. New York: Cambridge University Press.

BONNER, J. T., 1952. *Morphogenesis*. Princeton, N.J.: Princeton University Press.

BUCHSBAUM, R., 1948. *Animals without backbones*. Chicago: University of Chicago Press.

COTT, H. B., 1957. *Adaptive coloration in animals*. London: Methuen.

DARLINGTON, P. J., JR., 1958. *Zoogeography*. New York: Wiley.

GRIFFIN, D. R., 1962. *Animal structure and function*. New York: Holt, Rinehart and Winston, Inc. (In this series.)

HENDERSON, L. J., 1958. *The fitness of the environment*. Boston: Beacon Press.

HUXLEY, J. S., 1943. *Evolution. The modern synthesis*. New York: Harper.

JACOBS, W., 1954. *Fliegen, Schwimmen, Schweben*. Berlin: Springer.

LEVINE, R. P., 1962. *Genetics*. New York: Holt, Rinehart and Winston, Inc. (In this series.)

MAYR, E., 1963. *Animal species and evolution*. Cambridge, Mass.: Harvard University Press.

PROSSER, C. L., and BROWN, F. A., JR., 1961. *Comparative animal physiology*. Philadelphia: Saunders.

SAVAGE, J. M., 1963. *Evolution*. New York: Holt, Rinehart and Winston, Inc. (In this series.)

SCHMIDT-NIELSEN, K., 1960. *Animal physiology*. Englewood Cliffs, N.J.: Prentice-Hall.

WADDINGTON, C. H., 1962. *How animals develop*. New York: Harper.

WALLACE, B., and SRB., A. M., 1961. *Adaptation*. Englewood Cliffs, N.J.: Prentice-Hall.

WILSON, E. O., "Pheromones," *Scientific American*, May 1963, pp. 100–114.

CHAPTER THREE

A

CASE STUDY

IN RETROSPECT Adaptation is a multidimensional concept. Each dimension is important in its own right, but since all are inextricably interrelated, they must be appreciated collectively if a true biological grasp of the concept is to be achieved.

In the first chapter, we focused primarily on one dimension. We considered the mosquito and its various features—and some of them we looked at in great detail—but we gave no attention, or almost none, to other kinds of animals. We emerged with a good deal of interesting knowledge about an insect, which we might hitherto never have thought about, and perhaps we gained some satisfaction from spelling out in fairly concrete terms something that we were already intuitively predisposed to accept; namely, that there is nothing helter-skelter about an organism, and that each of its features, be it structural, functional, or behavioral, is neatly refined to meet the requisites of the animal's survival. An animal's features, in short, are adapted.

In the second chapter, another dimension was brought to light. This new dimension—the comparative dimension if you wish—is a most important one. We no longer looked at the mosquito by itself, but considered it in the context of the animal kingdom as a whole. Some sense could finally be made out of the bewildering array of its adaptations. A mosquito was now seen to be first and foremost a living animal, which like all others, does certain things that we have come to identify with animal life itself. It feeds, it excretes, it breathes, it reproduces. These are basic animal activities. The mosquito has its own special way of doing these things, and it has unique adaptive refinements, but the basic things it does are very much a part of animal life as a whole.

In a comparative context, every adaptive feature, no matter how trivial, may take on real meaning. Uric acid, the crystalline nitrogenous excretory product of the adult mosquito, was first viewed as just that: a peculiar excretory product. But once we learned that the same product is excreted by birds and lizards, then uric acid was seen as the nitrogenous waste product of animals whose mode of life requires that water be conserved to the utmost. By comparing, we learn to generalize, and by generalizing we are led to make predictions. Would an adult whirligig beetle, which spends much of its adult life in water, be expected to excrete uric acid, or would it excrete a water-rich urine with urea or ammonia? Since it has access to much water, the latter might be expected. Still, one wonders about the animal's reproductive behavior. How well does it fly, and how much time does it spend out of the water in search of a mate? If it spends much time out of water, might one not anticipate uric acid to be excreted? By predicting, we are providing a logical basis to the quest for further knowledge. We are now being truly scientific, for the method of the scientist is really nothing more than *an organized search for answers*. And for the biologist, organization most often finds its basis in comparative reasoning.

There is yet another dimension to adaptation, and this is a rather complex one. It might appropriately be called the "historical" dimension. How did an adaptation come into being? This is evidently not a simple question, and there is perhaps more than one valid way of interpreting it. We might be asking about the developmental basis of adaptation, and concern ourselves with the embryological history of the animal. Or we might be asking about the control of development, and be led on to think about the action of genes. This in turn would force us to consider the mechanism whereby a species maintains itself by reproducing in its own image; that is, by transmitting from generation to generation the blueprint of information (the genes) that controls the expression of its adaptive features. This, of course, is genetics. We would also have to face the fact that offspring are not produced in the *exact* image of their parents. The blueprint transmitted is not quite that of the parents. And there is great significance in this fact. For without a mechanism that ensures the maintenance of variability between individuals, a species would be doomed to extinction: it would lose its ability to "respond" adaptively to the shifting selective pressures of its environment. It would lose its ability to evolve.

Development, genetics, evolution—these are major fields of biological endeavor. But within the framework of this book we cannot extend ourselves to give each its deserved share of consideration; they are each treated at length in books by those titles in this series. An understanding of these fields is essential for a full appreciation of the dynamic nature of that which we call adaptation. Adaptations develop, are inherited, and evolve.

Let us here limit our approach by considering only one special aspect of this "historical" dimension that we have been talking about. If we accept the fact that organisms evolve—and the evidence is certainly overwhelming that they do—then each species can be viewed as something with a historical past. Every adaptation can itself be viewed in the light of its evolutionary history. An attempt to trace an ancestry is not an easy job, because critical past evolutionary stages are often extinct and have left no known fossil record. But fossils are not the only clues to evolution. There are other lines of evidence, often quite subtle, but equally useful. The fact of the matter is that over the past hundred years and more, a major portion of biologists' research efforts has gone into an attempt to reconstruct the history of the evolutionary unfolding of life on earth.

Suppose, then, that we were to tell in this chapter how the mosquito got to be what it is. What is its evolutionary ancestry? If we really wanted to begin at the beginning we would have to go back some two and a half billion years to the origins of life itself. We would begin by describing the conditions on earth before even the first organic molecules came into existence. A good deal of space would then have to be devoted to explaining how these organic molecules first formed spontaneously in the oceans, how they accumulated, why they were able to accumulate without decaying, how some of them came to form complex aggregates, and how eventually some of these aggregates became self-replicating evolving systems that one could truly call alive. We would then proceed to speculate on how the first cellular organisms might have arisen, how some of them developed the ability to photosynthesize, while others without the ability came to depend on those that had it. Those that photosynthesized gave rise to higher plants; those that did not, to animals. To get to the mosquito we would then follow the evolution of animals, considering first such ancestral forms as gave rise to sponges, coelenterates, flatworms, and then going on to speculate about the origin of the annelid superphylum—that vast array of creatures comprising present-day annelids, mollusks, arthropods, and some lesser known phyla. Within this complex of phyla we would have to focus attention on how arthropods arose from ancestral annelids, and eventually how the insects evolved within the arthropod phylum itself, and how they become the important terrestrial group they are today. Within the insects we would then attempt to trace the evolution of flies, and finally that of the mosquito itself.

The story would be a long one, and not a simple one to tell. Much of it would be speculative. Instead of giving you the full story, which would by necessity be oversimplified—and to some extent dangerously oversimplified because we could not take the space to give you the evidence—we shall focus instead on just one relatively minor phase of this long and involved evolutionary story. It is really not important which particular phase we pick. The point is to ask a question about some aspect of the evolutionary history of the mosquito, and then to proceed with you on a search for an answer. By going on this search, you will get a feeling for the kind of documentation of the evolutionary past that one can find, and for the ways of finding it. Evolutionary trees such as are commonly drawn in biology texts are based on the integrated answers to hundreds of individual inquiries of the type we are about to engage in, done by hundreds of different biologists at the investment of thousands of research hours.

What question shall we ask? How far back in the mosquito's ancestry shall we search for a topic of inquiry? Let us begin by looking at two phyla, the Annelida and the Arthropoda. On the one hand, the earthworms and their relatives, and on the other, the insects, millepedes, spiders, crustaceans, and the rest of their hard-shelled affiliates. There is general agreement among biologists of today that arthropods arose from some kind of ancestral annelid stock. You don't *have* to agree with this, but we should like you to believe that if we had more space in which to give supporting evidence, we could present you with a rather convincing case. Exactly what this ancestral annelid stock looked like nobody knows, for it has long since become extinct. (It might be fairer to say that nobody knew until quite recently, because, as we shall see presently, some very suggestive fossils have been discovered in the past few years in Australia.) Annelids and arthropods have a major characteristic in common: they are segmented. The very word "annelid" implies this fact, for Annelida means "the ringed ones," and ringed these worms certainly are (Fig. 3–1.) Think of an earthworm: its body is divided lengthwise into a series of segments. But arthropods also have their body divided into segments. True, this may be more apparent in some species than in others. The body of a millepede, for instance, resembles that of an earth-

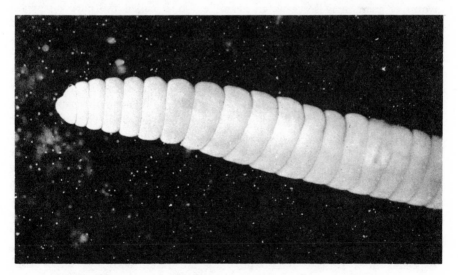

Fig. 3-1. Front end of an earthworm, showing conspicuous segmentation.

worm more than does, say, the body of a mosquito. But even in the mosquito, segmentation is clearly apparent, at least in the abdomen.

Let us now ask ourselves what the significance is of segmentation. Of what adaptive value is it for the animals that are segmented? Does segmentation have the same significance for the earthworm as it does for the millepede or the mosquito? What was the adaptive justification of segmentation when it first appeared in the early stages of annelid evolution? Might it not then have had different significance than it has for the modern forms alive today? These questions are not trivial, and can be asked of any adaptation in any organism or group of organisms. As regards segmentation in particular, we find the questions justifiable if for no other reason than that segmentation is a major feature shared by two enormously successful phyla. Let us proceed with this line of inquiry and look into the biological significance of segmentation in the annelids and in the arthropods.

SEGMENTATION IN TAPEWORMS AND CHORDATES

Segmentation has appeared twice independently in the course of animal evolution outside the annelid superphylum: in the tapeworms, and in the chordates. Of what significance is segmentation in these animals? Might these animals provide us with clues that could then help us in our original purpose of explaining segmentation in annelids and arthropods?

Let us first look at the situation in tapeworms. As is well known, tapeworms are all parasitic, and a familiar form, *Taenia solium,* the pork tapeworm of man, may serve as an example. (It is called the pork tapeworm because man acquires this intestinal parasite by eating improperly cooked pork in whose muscles the larval forms of the worm develop.) Tapeworms are highly adapted to a parasitic mode of life. They lack a digestive tract and absorb their food directly through their integument from the intestinal fluids of their host. They have no well-developed brain and possess no elaborate sense organs. At their front end they bear suckers (and sometimes also hooks, as in *T. solium*) by which they fasten themselves to the intestinal wall. The body of *Taenia* is divided lengthwise into segments (Fig. 3–2). Each segment is really a reproductive apparatus, complete with male and female organs. Mature segments, laden with fertile eggs, are continuously being shed at the tail end of the animal and voided with the feces of the host. These lost segments are replaced by new ones formed by an ever-active growth region in the "neck" of the animal. *Taenia* is thus seen as a truly formidable reproductive machine, turning out on an assembly-line basis one egg package after another. A high reproductive potential is certainly to be expected in a parasite whose offspring are faced with the rather risky prospects of having to invade two separate hosts before they in turn can

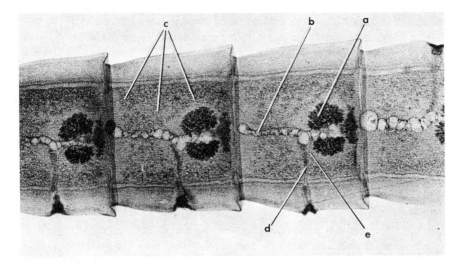

Fig. 3-2. Portion of a tapeworm (*Taenia pisiformis*). Each segment contains both male and female reproductive organs; a, ovary; b, uterus; c, testes; d, sperm duct; e, vagina.

mature and reproduce. Thus, the segmentation of tapeworms is distinctly a reproductive adaptation, one that can best be viewed in the light of the special demands of a parasitic mode of life. (Incidentally, the free-living relatives of tapeworms, such as planarians, have no more than the usual complement of reproductive organs and they are unsegmented. They also have a gut, brain, and elaborate sense organs.)

Segmentation in the chordates has entirely different significance. The chordates are an enormously varied group. It includes not only all vertebrates from fish to mammals, but also some lesser known groups that do not have vertebrae, such as the lancelets (*Amphioxus*), tunicates (Fig. 2–8), and certain wormlike forms that aren't worms at all. When we look at a vertebrate such as a frog, bird, or human being, there is nothing off-hand to suggest that these animals have any traits that are segmented. Certainly there are no obvious external signs of segmentation such as in an earthworm or tapeworm. But think of the skeleton. Aren't the vertebrae serially repeated? Also, isn't there a repetition of ganglia along most of the nerve cord? A fish is actually more suggestive because segmentation is clearly apparent even in the muscular system (think of a cooked fish, and of the discrete flakes of flesh arranged in series on both sides of the spine). In this arrangement of the musculature lies the very clue to what segmentation is all about in vertebrates. Segmentation is an adaptation to locomotion. When a fish swims, its body is thrown into undulations. Water is pushed back and the body is thrust forward. Waves of contraction sweep lengthwise over the muscles on each side of the body. The waves of the right are out of phase with those of the left—hence the undulations. The arrangement of the muscles intc serially aligned units reflects the very nature of their segmental activity. One can now also account for why the nerve cord consists of a chain of ganglia; it makes sense for the spatial arrangement of the ganglia to parallel that of the muscle units whose activity they control. And what about the vertebral nature of the spine? The prime function of a skeleton is to provide support, but it must do so without undue restriction of mobility. A chain of articulated skeletal units arranged along a central axis provides just that for an undulating fish. It seems clear, therefore, that in vertebrates—or at least in fish—the segmental features of musculature, nervous system, and skeleton can be justified as adaptations to a special type of locomotion. The adaptive significance of segmentation here is obviously quite different from what it is in a tapeworm.

In the "higher" vertebrates, comprising the land-dwelling descendants of fish—the amphibians, reptiles, birds, and mammals—the methods of locomotion have departed quite radically from that of fish. This is because the colonization of land brought about an increased dependence on the appendages for support and for locomotion. The body plan of the ancestral fish underwent some fairly radical anatomical changes. Specialized appendages require for their proper operation specialized muscles, as well as a specialized skeletal framework. The muscles of the legs of an antelope are disposed quite differently from those that operate the fins of a fish. There is no true foot, thigh, or shank in a fish fin. Nor does the fish show the elaborate skeletal specializations (the pectoral and pelvic girdles) that are indispensable for bracing the burdened appendages of a land dweller against its spine. It is apparent, therefore, that in higher vertebrates, the primitive segmental features that are so clearly apparent in fish have become somewhat obscured simply because these higher vertebrates no longer move like their aquatic ancestors.

But does a fish really illustrate the primitive type of chordate locomotion? Probably yes. We know from indisputable fossil evidence what the immediate vertebrate ancestors of modern fish looked like. They were generally fishlike in appearance, although they lacked jaws and paired fins, and were probably mudgrubbers. They wiggled along by body undulations like those of modern fish, but unlike the latter, which can swim freely and can control their rolling motion with their paired fins, they probably spent their life confined to the bottom. It might be mentioned incidentally that there are still direct descendants of these ancestral mudgrubbers alive in the world today. Among them are the lampreys (Fig. 3–3). A lamprey has no paired fins and no jaws. In this respect it is primitive. But it has become highly specialized in other respects. Unlike its ancestors, it is an ectoparasite that feeds on other fish, attaching itself to their body surface and sucking their blood and body fluids (it is one of these same lampreys that has become such a menace to the commercial fishing industry of the Great Lakes).

Fig. 3-3. Lamprey parasitic on catfish. (Courtesy of the American Museum of Natural History.)

But did not these jawless, finless fish themselves have ancestors? What were these like, and how did they move? After all, if we wish to claim that the segmental features of vertebrates evolved in adaptation to a type of locomotion essentially no different from that of modern fish, then we should at least attempt to find out whether the earliest chordates indeed moved like fish. Unfortunately, the fossil record is of no help in telling us what these ancestral chordates looked like. But something can be learned from such modern-day forms as lancelets and tunicates that have apparently descended directly from them. The lancelet, *Amphioxus*, for instance, is really rather fishlike in appearance (Fig. 3–4). Its muscles are segmentally arranged, and there is a nerve cord running dorsally the length of the body. There is no spine in the true sense of the word, although in its place there is a flexible rod called the notochord that has the same skeletal function of a spine. Thus, except for the lack of vertebrae, the lancelet really has all those features of a fish that we have been calling segmental. Its locomotion is also fishlike. True, it spends much of its time partly buried in sand, but when swimming about, its body wiggles like that of a fish. Other "invertebrate chordates," such as the tunicates, are sessile as adults, but their immatures are motile forms similar to tadpoles in appearance, and endowed with an undulatory tail (Fig. 2–8). Some biologists argue that the ancestral chordates might have had a life cycle like that of modern tunicates, that is, with sessile adults and motile larvae. Whether or not this is true, it seems clear that they were fishlike in at least one stage of their life cycle. And it was this stage—

muscle segments

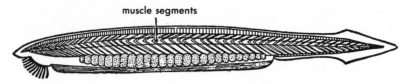

Fig. 3-4. *Amphioxus,* showing the segmental arrangement of the musculature. (From Wilder, *History of the Human Body,* Holt, Rinehart and Winston, Inc.)

which moved by undulations, and which had its musculature, nervous system, and skeletal system adapted accordingly—that was eventually preserved as the exclusive stage in fish and in all other subsequent lineages of vertebrate evolution.

SEGMENTATION IN ANNELID WORMS; LOCOMOTION

So much for tapeworms and chordates; let us now look into the reasons for segmentation in annelid worms. We can momentarily ignore the arthropods. After all, segmentation was not acquired by anthropods on their own, but is something they inherited from annelid ancestors, and it is thus only logical to ponder first how segmentation came into being in the older of the two groups. We can immediately rule out the possibility that segmentation in annelids evolved for similar reasons as in tapeworms. Annelids are a free-living group, and the only parasitic forms, the leeches, are parasitic in a very different way from tapeworms: they attach themselves to the outside of their hosts, rather than living in their insides, and moreover do so only when feeding, spending the rest of their time living free. Also, the body plan of a leech has departed quite radically from that of its more primitive annelid ancestors.

What about locomotion? Is segmentation in annelids justifiable on the same grounds as in chordates? How do annelids move? And which of their anatomical features are actually segmented?

If we dissected an annelid such as an earthworm, one of the first things that would strike us as reminiscent of a chordate is the nerve cord. It consists of a chain of regularly spaced ganglia, one to each body segment. It is not situated dorsally as in chordates, but lies ventrally, beneath the gut. This difference is evidence for the two groups having acquired this type of nerve cord independently from one another. By inference from what we learned from chordates we might reason that a segmental spacing of ganglia in the earthworm means one thing: that its locomotion is in some way dependent on a musculature that is similarly divided into segmental units. There is indeed a well-developed musculature in the earthworm; in fact, the bulk of its body wall is made of muscle fibers. These are arranged into two layers: an outer one of circular fibers, and an inner one of longitudinal fibers (Fig. 3–5). And, as we shall see shortly, the muscles of each segment do indeed behave as functional units. Of course, there is one radical anatomical difference between an earthworm and a chordate. The earthworm is soft and pliable, whereas the chordate has an obvious skeleton. But is this difference so radical? Is the earthworm *really* without a skeleton? The fact of the matter is that the earthworm has a very good skeleton. It is not a skeleton made of bone, but one made of liquid. It is a so-called hydrostatic skeleton. To understand what we mean by this, we must take a closer look at the earthworm's anatomy.

If we were to slice an earthworm lengthwise in half (Fig. 3–5), we would see that the animal really consists of a tube within a tube. The inner tube is the gut, the outer one is the muscular body wall. Between the two tubes is the fluid-filled body cavity, or coelom. The important thing to note is that this cavity is divided up along its length by a series of transverse partitions, or *septa*. These are quite regularly spaced and actually denote the very junction of the segments. The septa are fluid-tight. There is a hole in each septum where the nerve cord goes through, but even here a snug fit is maintained by a special sphincter in the septum itself.

Suppose we think of a single segment and imagine what would happen if either the circular or the longitudinal muscles of the body wall were to contract. Contraction of the circular fibers would cause the segment to con-

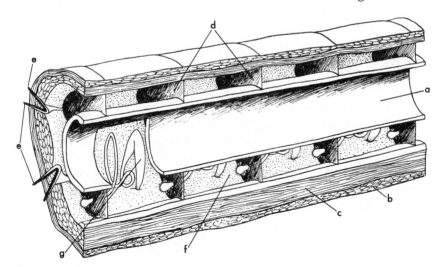

Fig. 3-5. Portion of an earthworm, sliced lengthwise in half (circulatory and nervous systems omitted); a, gut; b, circular muscles; c, longitudinal muscles; d, septa; e, chaetae; f, coelomic cavity; g, nephridium. (Courtesy of D. W. Alsop and F. A. McKittrick.)

strict and lengthen. The longitudinal fibers would do the exact opposite: the segment would shorten and increase in girth. The two muscles can evidently act as antagonists to one another; that is, if they were to operate out of phase, each can, by its contraction, restore the other to the stretched condition. Such antagonistic action would be impossible without the septa. Suppose the septa were not there, and that the coelomic fluid were free to slosh in all directions. If the circular muscles of a segment contracted, there would be a local constriction but no significant lengthening at that point: the coelomic fluid would simply squirt fore and aft, instead of pressing against the septa and stretching the segment. Similarly, contraction of the longitudinal fibers would bring about a local shortening but no major increase in girth. Antagonistic sets of muscles are quite common in animals. Our own limbs, for instance, operate under the action of antagonists. The arm is flexed by the biceps, and it is extended by antagonists on the opposite side of the arm. It is the skeleton that makes such antagonistic action possible, since its relation to the muscles is such as to assure that when one contracts, the other is stretched. In an earthworm it is the trapped liquid between the septa that enables the circular and longitudinal muscles of a segment to act as antagonists. In that sense, this liquid may be thought of as fulfilling a skeletal role. And that is why we speak of the compartmentalized coelom of an earthworm as consisting of a hydrostatic skeleton. Let us now see how all of this relates to the actual locomotion of an earthworm.

In Fig. 3–6 are shown four consecutive stages in the normal crawling activity of an earthworm. Some of the segments have been numbered so that their position can be followed from stage to stage. Notice that there are certain regions that are swollen and others that are constricted. Notice, moreover, that the segmental composition of these regions is not fixed, but changes as the animal moves along: what is a swelling at one time becomes a constriction at another, and vice versa. What is happening is that waves of contraction are propagated along the length of the worm, involving alternately the circular and the longitudinal musculature of the segments. Each segment is thus seen to go through a continuing cycle of activity, in which the two sets of muscles contract in regular alternation. When the longitudinal muscles contract, the segment is part of a swelling; when the circular muscles contract, it is part of a constriction. Coordination between segments is such that adjacent ones are just a bit out of phase. The result (see Fig. 3–6) is that segments at the front of each swelling move forward to become part of a constricted zone, and those at the front of a constricted zone add to the rear of the swelling ahead; thus the worm inches forward. The process is really a bit more complicated, for the swollen regions are actually anchored to the substrate by sets of extrusible bristles called *chaetae* (Fig. 3–5), but the essentials of locomotion are as described. Incidentally, the mechanism of locomotion is much the same when the worm is burrowing instead of crawling.

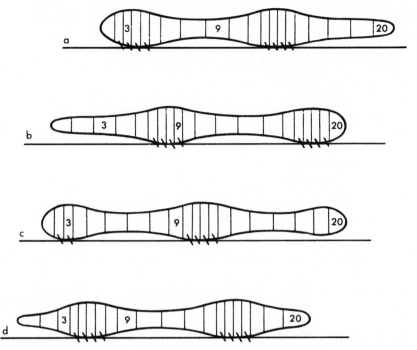

Fig. 3-6. Consecutive stages in the locomotion of an earthworm. See text for details. (From Ramsay, *A Physiological Approach to the Lower Invertebrates*, Cambridge University Press.)

The role of the compartmentalized coelom is clear: without a hydrostatic skeleton the individual segments could not operate as the functional units they in fact are. All three major systems—skeletal, muscular, and nervous—are structurally patterned to conform to the demands of a special type of locomotion. The parallel with chordates is obvious, but should not be exploited for more than its worth. Although in both earthworm and fishlike chordates the same three anatomical systems are the ones to show segmentation, and although their locomotion is similar in that it depends on waves of contraction sweeping over segmentally arranged muscles, the details of the anatomy and the exact mode of locomotion in the two are sufficiently distinct to rule out the possibility that annelids and chordates are immediately related to one another. There are also many other lines of convincing evidence that speak against the two groups being closely related.

Other Features of the Earthworm

So far we have concerned ourselves only with the muscular, nervous, and skeletal systems of an earthworm, and have ignored all of its other anatomical features. Let us briefly consider also the circulatory and the excretory systems. But before we actually look at the worm itself, let us see if we can predict what these systems might be like.

The very fact that the body cavity is compartmentalized has important implications. Recall the body cavity of the mosquito. The fluid in it is the mosquito's blood, and there is no reason why it cannot serve for transport of materials, since the body cavity is an open system uninterrupted by partitions. But in an earthworm, how could material absorbed from the gut in one region be distributed to organs elsewhere in the body if the coelomic fluid were the only means of conveyance? If there is to be an effective transport system, something other than the body cavity must provide the means. It is therefore not unexpected that the earthworm should have a well-developed closed circulatory system. There is a dorsal vessel and a ventral vessel, and segmental ramifications of these penetrate all the major organ systems. Although there is no centralized heart, many of the vessels, including the entire dorsal vessel, are contractile, and effectively pump the blood along (Fig. 3–7).

There is yet another implication to coelom compartmentalization. Think of the excretory demands of the animal. Are not the coelomic sacs potentially stagnant pools in which waste products from the surrounding tissues might be expected to accumulate? How might provision be made for eliminating such wastes? One way would be to send into the coelomic chambers loops of capillary blood vessels into which the wastes could diffuse. A kidney, properly associated with the circulation elsewhere in the body, could then remove these wastes from the blood and pass them to the outside. Or, instead of

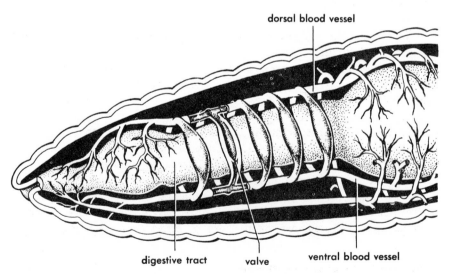

dorsal blood vessel

digestive tract   valve   ventral blood vessel

Fig. 3-7. Circulation in the front end of an earthworm (diagrammatic). The capillaries that ordinarily join the major vessels are too small to be visible at this scale. (From Griffin, *Animal Structure and Function,* Holt, Rinehart and Winston, Inc.)

sending capillaries into each chamber, some kind of direct communication might be maintained between the blood and the fluid in the chambers, so that the fluid is actually taken continuously into the circulation, passed by a kidney, and then returned in a purified condition to the chambers. Both of these solutions are, admittedly, cumbersome, but if the latter seems ridiculously farfetched, do some reading on the relationship of blood and lymph in vertebrates. There is a third solution to the problem: an earthworm could rely on individual excretory organs installed in each compartment. The so-called nephridia are just that. There are two per segment (Fig. 3–5). Each is a slender coiled tube, opening at one end into the coelom by a ciliated funnel, and directly to the outside at the other end. They serve to discharge, in addition to excretory wastes, the excess water that diffuses into the worm from the moist soil around it. Oddly, the nephridia of each segment have their ciliated intake in the segment immediately in front. (Can you think of one or perhaps several functional justifications for this arrangement?)

The body plan of an earthworm thus seems to reflect a rather "logical" state of affairs. Everything about the worm makes "sense" in terms of everything else. It is quite easy, once we know some parts of it, to predict what some of the rest should be like. A word of caution is in order here, lest more meaning be read into the word "logical" than was intended. By first singling out for study certain of the organ systems and then predicting the structure of others, we did not wish to imply that the structures evolved in that same sequence; that is, that there was first a compartmentalized coelom, and that subsequently a circulatory system "had" to evolve, and segmental nephridia "had" to evolve. In evolution, nothing ever appears in anticipation of the later evolution of something else. If a structure is not in its own right compatible with life when it first appears, then it will simply not be retained and passed to subsequent generations by the species that acquires it. Neither do we mean that all the features we discussed in the earthworm evolved concurrently; some of them might have, others probably did not. The relative evolutionary age of the structural components of an organism cannot be estimated from looking at that organism alone. The organism must be compared with others. With the earthworm we are about to do just that—and for more reasons than this one.

Other Annelids

We are trying to establish the adaptive justification for segmentation in annelids. We have now worked with an earthworm, and our conclusion has been that in this animal segmentation is best interpreted in terms of locomotion. What we do not know yet is the extent to which earthworms resemble those ancestral annelids in which segmentation first appeared. What were these ancestral worms like? Did they move like earthworms? Did they have a compartmentalized coelom? Were their other segmental features also like those of earthworms? There are two things we could do to answer these questions. First, we could compare earthworms with other living annelids. If there is general uniformity within the phylum, at least as regards segmentation and type of locomotion, then we might suspect that we are dealing with basic characteristics of long evolutionary standing. Second, we could examine whatever annelids are known from the fossil record. We shall follow both of these courses.

Annelids constitute a big and varied group. The overwhelming majority of them are aquatic. This is not surprising, since most invertebrate phyla have apparently arisen in the ocean (life itself almost certainly arose in the ocean) and nearly all of them still have marine representatives. Assuming that the annelids are also primitively marine, then an earthworm is seen to be a somewhat specialized form, certainly to the extent that it has made the transition to a semiterrestrial mode of life. We say semiterrestrial rather than terrestrial because an earthworm is really restricted to moisture-laden soil and cannot long withstand dryness. Marine annelids are therefore likely to include the older members of the phylum, and it is to them that we should turn in our search for clues to what ancestral annelids might have been like.

Neanthes

The marine annelids comprise an enormous group, technically known as the Polychaeta. It is difficult to give a true idea of how diverse a group this really is. Polychaetes include some of the most stunningly beautiful animals of the ocean, and they are often so bizarre that they are hardly recognizable as worms. Many of them live in tubes that they themselves manufacture. Others burrow in sand. The tube dwellers frequently have their front ends adorned with tentacles that give them the appearance of corals or sea anemones (Fig. 3–8). For our present purposes we shall single out a polychaete whose appearance is such that one would unhesitatingly call it an annelid worm at first glance. The species is one that is probably known to some of you since it is an excellent and widely used fishing bait. It is the common clamworm of our North Atlantic coast. We shall henceforth refer to it by its generic name, *Neanthes* (Fig. 3–9).

Neanthes is a big worm, commonly a foot long, but sometimes even achieving twice this length. Neatly arranged on each side of the animal is a series of fleshy lobes, beset with bristles, called *parapodia*. These structures are absent in the earthworm, and since they are segmentally arranged—there is a pair of parapodia per segment—their presence will evidently have to be explained. If we were to dissect the worm, we would find ourselves confronted with a rather familiar anatomical layout. A gut runs the length of the animal. There is a muscular body wall, and there is a coelomic cavity with septa stretched across it. There is a ventral nerve cord, a closed circulatory system, and paired nephridia. On close examination we would notice, however, that things are not quite what they were in an earthworm. First, and this is very important, the septa are imperfect, being conspicuously perforated. We are evidently dealing with an animal whose locomotion cannot possibly be exactly like that of an earthworm. Other differences would also soon become apparent. There are special muscles whose disposition suggests that they must impart some kind of movement to the parapodia. Even the muscles of the body wall are somewhat peculiar. There is an outer layer of circular fibers as in an earthworm, but the inner longitudinal fibers, rather than being distributed more or less evenly around the whole body, are lumped into four discrete longitudinal bands, two dorsolateral ones, and two ventrolateral ones. There is a cuticle surrounding the entire animal. Although flexible, it is considerably tougher than that of an earthworm; so much so, in fact, that the girth of the animal is fixed and there can be no swelling or constriction such as in a moving earthworm (Fig. 3–10).

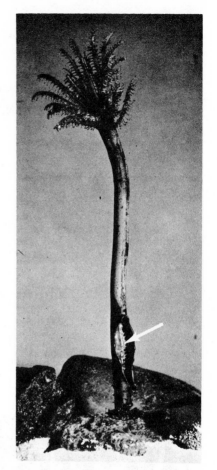

Fig. 3-8. *Sabella:* a tube-dwelling polychaete. The front end, beset with feathery gills, protrudes from the tube. The gills are slimy and entrap small organisms that are then conveyed to the mouth by cilia. The slender body of the worm is visible (arrow) where the tube has been dissected open. (Photograph of a glass model.)

These anatomical peculiarities take on meaning when we examine the living worm and how it moves. Actually, *Neanthes* does not move about very much at all. It spends most of its time confined to burrows that it builds in sandy or muddy sea bottom. It lies in its burrow, with its head at the opening, occasionally protruding its front end in search for food. It has a pair of strong horny jaws that it exposes by everting its pharynx, and with which it can seize and pull food (including live prey) back into its burrow. The water in the burrow is kept from stagnating by intermittent undulations of the worm's body. The incoming water not only serves to

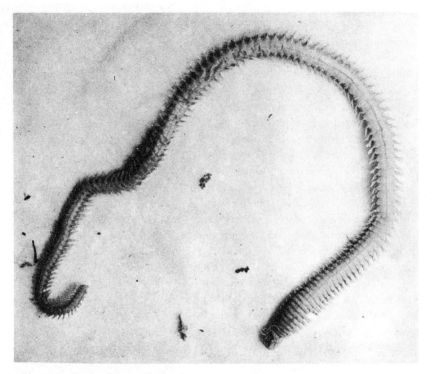

A

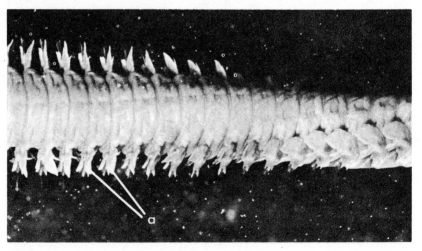

B

Fig. 3-9. A: *Neanthes;* B: Enlarged view of small section of worm, showing parapodia, a.

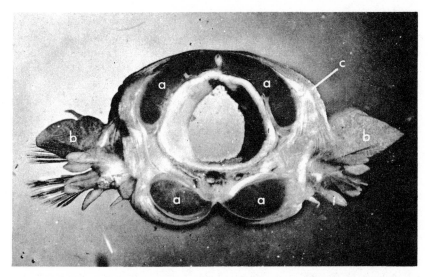

Fig. 3-10. Cross section of *Neanthes*. Note the four bundles of powerful longitudinal muscles, a; b, parapodia; c, cuticle.

renew the oxygen supply, but may also be the source of chemical clues that alert the worm to the presence of food nearby.

Neanthes leaves its burrow on its own initiative during the breeding season, but may also be forced to move elsewhere when food in the area becomes scarce or when a calamity destroys its burrow. When on the move, *Neanthes* can either crawl or swim. Crawling is accomplished by a paddle-like action of the parapodia, which are seen to move rhythmically back and forth. During the backstroke, which is the effective stroke, the parapodium is maintained protruded and is bent a bit downward so that it sweeps back against the substrate. During the recovery stroke, the parapodium is raised and slightly retracted. The parapodia do not operate in synchrony. One gets the impression when observing the worm that waves of activity are sweeping lengthwise over the parapodia of each side, with the waves of opposite sides being in alternation to one another. Thus, each parapodium is, at any one stage in its cycle, just a bit out of phase with its neighbors, and precisely out of phase with its segmental partner.

Neanthes can shift over to a more rapid crawl by superimposing on its parapodial activity lateral undulations of the body itself. The undulations, reminiscent of those of fish, are brought about by waves of contraction propagated alternately along the longitudinal muscle bundles of the right and left sides of the body. *Neanthes* can also swim freely with considerable agility, and its movements here are much the same as in rapid crawling; that is, the worm makes use of parapodial paddling in combination with body undulations, the only difference being that in swimming the undulatory waves are of greater amplitude.

Which is more truly representative of the ancestral condition, *Neanthes* or an earthworm? With the evidence at hand we can arrive at no definite answer. The two worms are clearly different, despite the fundamental similarity of their body plans. In the earthworm, the entire anatomical layout as well as the animal's locomotion made such good sense in terms of coelom compartmentalization that we came to regard this compartmentalization as the central feature of annelid segmentation. And now, here we are with *Neanthes*, an animal that by virtue of its marine habits alone might be taken to be rather close to the ancestral annelid stock, and it turns out not to have a compartmentalized coelom at all! The septa are there, but they are perforated. Does this mean that our ideas will have to be discarded altogether? It certainly looks as though they might have to be. But let us first give the matter some more thought.

What is really so peculiar about *Neanthes* that sets it off from an earthworm? In addition to the imperfect septa, there are the parapodia with their special muscles, a longitudinal musculature grouped into bundles, and a tough body cuticle that maintains the animal strait-jacketed and prevents local changes in body girth such as are necessary for an earthworm's type of locomotion. Let us for the moment entertain a modified version of our hypothesis, no matter how farfetched the added assumptions might seem at first. Suppose that the characteristics of *Neanthes* are really secondary characteristics, and that the earthworm, despite its emigration from the ancestral habitat, has actually retained much more closely the primitive annelid body plan. In other words, let us suppose that a compartmentalized coelom and the earthworm's type of locomotion (or something closely similar) are really primitive characteristics, and that *Neanthes* represents a form that—by some reason that will have to be explained—has departed fundamentally from the original condition; obviously, we will also have to explain the earthworm's failure to depart from this condition.

Before we go any further, we should first examine some other polychaetes. We should, after all, make certain that *Neanthes* is not some kind of evolutionary oddity, and that most other polychaetes do not in fact resemble earthworms rather closely. We would quickly find that they do not. This is not to say that they all look alike and look like *Neanthes*; nothing could be further from the truth. We have already emphasized the extraordinary diversity of the polychaetes, and how totally unwormlike some of them may be in appearance. But there is one overriding fact that is of central importance to our argument. Those particular features of *Neanthes* that have been of specific concern to us are by no means peculiar to *Neanthes*, but are rather generally possessed by polycheates as a whole. Parapodia, for one thing, are a most basic polychaete attribute. Not all species use them as locomotory paddles; they sometimes serve as gills, or they may be used to create currents that sweep food particles into a worm's tube, or they may help the worm control its movements in its tube, or—and this is not unusual—they may serve in the same animal for several of these functions (in *Neanthes*, for instance, the parapodia might evidently also serve as gills since they are well irrigated by blood vessels). The possession of imperfect septa is also by no means a rarity. Sometimes there may be no traces of septa in most or even all of the adult body. Before we go on, let us examine one other polychaete.

Arenicola

According to Webster's dictionary, one meaning of the verb "to lug" is "to drag along with difficulty." *Arenicola marina*, the so-called lugworm of our North Atlantic coast, does justice to its name (Fig. 3–11). It inhabits areas of muddy sand close to shore, where it lives within U-shaped burrows of its own construction. In Chapter 2 we briefly discussed *Arenicola's* blood pigment. The worm is a powerful animal, exquisitely adapted for digging, but when removed from its burrow it is quite helpless. It can swim but very feebly, and cannot crawl effectively at all.

There is nothing spectacular about the worm as seen from the outside. Parapodia are found along much of the length of the body, although they are reduced and quite different in appearance from the "paddles" of *Neanthes*. On its mid-portion the animal has a series of paired gills. The body wall is strongly muscled in the usual annelid way. The more interesting features are to be found on the inside of the animal. The almost complete lack of

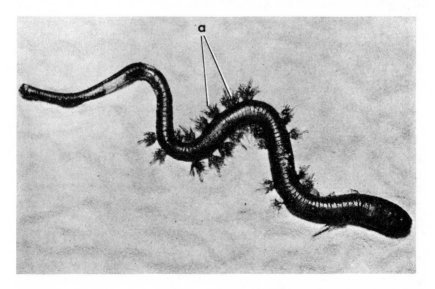

Fig. 3-11. *Arenicola*, removed from its burrow; a, gills. (Photograph of a glass model.)

septa is instantly apparent when the worm is opened (Fig. 3–12A). There are three imperfect septa at the anterior end, and a series at the tail end (Fig. 3–12B), but the remainder of the cavity is an open unpartitioned space. The digestive and circulatory systems are essentially as usual, but the nephridia are of interest in that they are relatively few in number (only six pairs). It is as if a reduction in their number had occurred because in the absence of a compartmentalized coelom there was no longer a justification for retaining a full complement of them. This, of course, implies that complete septation was the primitive rather than the derived condition, and so far we do not really know that this was the case.

The lack of septa explains *Arenicola's* inability to crawl in the manner of an earthworm. *Arenicola* is really fit only for burrowing, and it does so by using its eversible pharynx as a spearhead. By contracting the longitudinal body muscles, it engenders a force that, transmitted by the coelomic fluid and deployed forward, causes the pharynx to evert and to be thrust forcibly into the sand ahead. As the pharynx is then retracted, the worm moves forward into the space provided. The pharynx literally carves a way for the worm to follow. Locomotion is entirely different from that of the burrowing earthworm, and is dependent on the controlled deployment of pressure generated in a body cavity that is for all intents and purposes a single sac of fluid. The feeding mechanism of *Arenicola* is essentially similar to the burrowing mechanism, the only difference being that the everted pharynx, rather than being retracted empty, is withdrawn with a full load of sand. The worm feeds primarily from sand that slides from the surface down the main shaft of its U-shaped burrow. (In passing, see if you can explain the presence of a relatively large number of septa at the tail end of the worm. It has been suggested that without them the worm would have difficulty defecating. Why would this be the case? Can you think of other functional justifications for these caudal septa?)

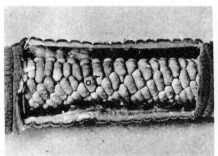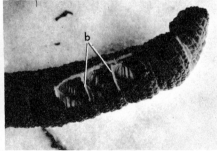

A   B

Fig. 3-12. A: Mid-body portion of *Arenicola,* with window cut in body wall. There are no septa connecting the gut, a, to the body wall. B: Similar view of terminal segments. Note septa, b.

We could go on and examine still other polychaetes, but we should be hard put to find species with a completely septated coelom like that of an earthworm. In polychaetes, complete septation is simply not the rule. What we should attempt to determine is whether this is the primitive or the derived condition. Are modern-day polychaetes the "simplified" descendants of a fully septated stock, and do earthworms represent relatively unmodified direct descendants of this stock? Or was the ancestral stock nonseptated, and has coelom compartmentalization evolved gradually by piecemeal addition of septa? In other words, might there at first have been a partially septate coelom as in *Arenicola*, then a complete set of imperfect septa as in *Neanthes*, and finally the perfcct fluid-tight partitions of earthworms? Although we are distinctly biased in favor of the first of the two alternatives, we should continue gathering whatever evidence might be obtainable. What does the fossil record tell us about ancestral annelids? Unfortunately, there is a limit to what one can learn from fossils, and the two things that are most critical for us—the internal anatomy and the mode of locomotion—are likely to be difficult, if not impossible, to determine from fossils.

Fossil evidence

Until very recently, the oldest known fossil annelids were from a certain rock formation from British Columbia called the Burgess Shale. These fossils date back over 500 million years to the middle of the geologic period known as the Cambrian. As old as these worms are, the remarkable thing about them is that they already had some of the fundamental characteristics of the polychaetes of today (Fig. 3–13A). Parapodia, for instance, were present, and their similarity to those of *Neanthes* suggests that they were probably used in much the same way. Clearly, these worms did not move like earthworms, and they need not have had a fully compartmentalized coelom. But are these really the "ancestral" annelids we are looking for? The origin of annelids must go back well into Precambrian times. That this is true is written in the Burgess Shale itself, for in this shale there are already present, besides the annelids, a wealth of arthropod types. Crustaceans are there, as well as a variety of representatives of other arthropod groups that are now extinct. What we want to know is what annelids were like *before* they gave rise to arthropods. The only thing the Burgess Shale tells us is that polychaetes changed relatively little since the Cambrian. It tells us nothing about the changes undergone by the worms before the Cambrian. And there is no reason why before the Cambrian these worms might not have had an elaborate evolutionary history. Competition with their own arthropod descendants might in itself have had important consequences on the course of their evolution. Arthropods, with their exoskeleton and versatile jointed appendages, must have been rather formidable competitors for the early annelids to have had to contend with. Perhaps annelids were even the chief food of early arthropods. It is therefore entirely conceivable that arthropods, when

A   B

Fig. 3-13. Fossils from the Burgess Shale. A: *Canadia setigera,* a polychaete. B: *Aysheaia pedunculata,* an onychophore. (From Kummel, *History of the Earth,* W. H. Freeman and Co., 1961. Courtesy of the publishers, and of H. B. Whittington, who took the pictures.)

they first appeared, caused the extinction of many an ancestral annelid type, and that only those annelids that were properly adapted to withstand this competition survived to leave their imprint in the Burgess Shale.

We can draw a parallel here. You will recall that the ancestral vertebrates were mudgrubbing fishlike forms without jaws or fins. These forms later became extinct, and it is most probable that their very own descendants were largely responsible for forcing their extinction. These descendants, with paired fins and jaws, were good swimmers and many of them probably were effective predators. In their presence, their less agile progenitors must have been at a great disadvantage—a disadvantage that in the long run was to prove insurmountable for the majority of them. Only a very few forms, including the lampreys, withstood this competition and survived to become part of the fauna of today. For the lamprey, the key to survival might have been its radical departure from the ancestral feeding habits: it became a parasite on some of the very fish that were destined to replace its relatives (Fig. 3–3). A lamprey is thus seen to be a rather paradoxical creature, primitive in its lack of jaws and fins, and highly specialized in its parasitic habits. When we are confronted with the polychaetes of the Burgess Shale we wonder to what extent these are similarly paradoxical. Some of their traits might be primitive, having been carried over unchanged from annelid progenitors of prearthropod times, but others are likely to have evolved only later, when the arthropods became a major selective factor in the annelid's environment. The unsolved question is, which are the older traits and which are the more recently acquired ones? With the lamprey this question could be answered simply by contrasting this animal with known fossil progenitors dating back to a time when fish with jaws and fins had not yet come into being. But we cannot answer the question as it applies to annelids, because we do not know what these worms were like before the advent of arthropods. The Burgess Shale certainly did not give us the answer. We need fossils from Precambrian times. But before we see what Precambrian fossils are like, let us turn to an entirely different line of evidence that does not involve fossils at all.

Embryological evidence

When we compare organisms for the purpose of determining their evolutionary relationships, we need not rely exclusively on what we can learn from the adults. Sometimes the immature forms—including even the earliest embryonic stages—offer extremely valuable clues to an organism's affinities. Take, for instance, the case of echinoderms and chordates. If we were to tell you that the echinoderms have closer affinities with the chordates than with any other living phylum of animals, you might justifiably be somewhat skeptical at first, since there is, after all, not a single echinoderm that resembles a chordate even remotely. But this dissimilarity applies only to adults. It is a fact that there is an extraordinary closeness of appearance between larvae of some echinoderms and those of certain chordates (the Hemichordata, a group of "invertebrate" chordates). Other bits of evidence also speak for the affinities of chordates and echinoderms, but this larval similarity is one of the most convincing. We could cite other examples involving groups of organisms that, despite pronounced evolutionary divergence of their adult forms, have retained closely similar immature stages. In the vertebrates, for instance, the early embryos are remarkably alike in all groups. Thus it is that an early human embryo has a tail and gill pouches just as those of a young fish embryo (Fig. 3–14). We do not mean to imply by these examples that there is invariably closer similarity between developmental stages than between adults. The exact opposite is sometimes true: evolution has sometimes emphasized divergence of larval rather than of adult forms. For instance, the maggot of a fly such as one is likely to find in decaying flesh is quite unlike a mosquito larva in appearance, yet adult fly and mosquito are relatively similar. The difference in larvae reflects the difference in larval habitats, just as similarity of adults reflects similarity of adult habitats.

What does this have to do with annelids? The point is the following. Suppose that in the evolution of polychaetes, as in that of vertebrates, it was the *adult* form that underwent the greater evolutionary change, and that the early developmental stages remained relatively unchanged. If this is true, could one, by examining the early developmental stages of modern polychaetes, get a clue as to whether ancestral annelids did or did not have a compartmentalized coelom? If, as we suspect, ancestral Precambrian annelids

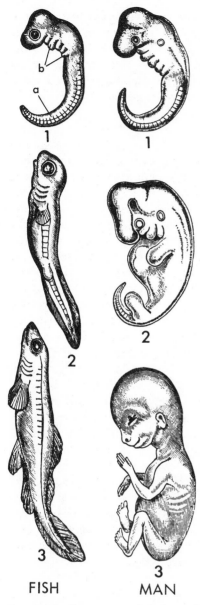

Fig. 3-14. Comparison of embryonal stages of fish and man. Note the similarity of the early stage in which tail, a, and gill pouches, b, are present in both. (From Romanes, *Darwin and After Darwin*, Open Court Publishing Company.)

did have a full set of perfect septa, then might it not be that a modern polychaete still builds such a full set of septa early in its embryology—just as did the embryo of its presumed ancestor —and that it is only later in its development that these septa become perforated (as in *Neanthes*) or that most of them disappear altogether (as in *Arenicola*)? Let us investigate this possibility by studying the actual course of polychaete embryology.

Fertilization in most polychaetes occurs outside their own bodies in the sea water itself. The fertilized egg undergoes a series of divisions, the daughter cells differentiate, and there is formed a tiny ciliated larva called the trochophore (Fig. 3–15). It is a poor swimmer and moves with the plankton at the mercy of the prevailing currents; but despite its obvious vulnerability it is a most important stage in the life cycle of a polychaete, for it is through this readily dispersed form that each new crop of offspring is given a chance to drift away from the potentially crowded region of its birth. The trochophore is a remarkably complex little organism but need not be described here in detail. Note, however, that it already has a digestive tract complete with mouth and anus. The space between the gut and body wall is the so-called primary body cavity or *blastocoel*. (This term is generally used to denote the first-formed space between endoderm and ectoderm in a developing embryo or larva.)

The beginnings of the transformation from trochophore larva to adult worm occur before the larva abandons its pelagic existence (Fig. 3–15). A cylindrical process, destined to become the body of the adult worm, grows downward from the perianal region of the trochophore. This outgrowth carries with it an extension of the gut itself, so that the anus remains at all times at the tip of the outgrowth. Two strips of undifferentiated tissue are seen to flank the gut along its full length within the outgrowth. These strips, which constitute the so-called mesoderm (one of the three fundamental embryonic tissue layers) are laid down by the continuing division of a single pair of cells (Fig. 3–15e) that lie just inside the tip of the outgrowth. The cells in the two strips of mesoderm become grouped into a series of clumps, so that each strip assumes a roughly beaded appearance. At the same time, transverse annulations appear along the body wall, and the adult segmental pattern is laid down. One pair of mesodermal cell clumps lies in each segment. A remarkable thing happens next. Within the center of each meso-dermal clump, the cells part to form a small cavity. The cavity enlarges and each clump now becomes a fluid-filled pouch. What we are witnessing here are the beginnings of coelom formation. The two pouches in each segment continue to expand, gradually obliterating the entire space (blastocoel) be-tween gut and body wall. Eventually the pouches make contact with one another above and below the gut, as well as with neighbors from the seg-ments in front and behind. Where they meet, cellular partitions are formed:

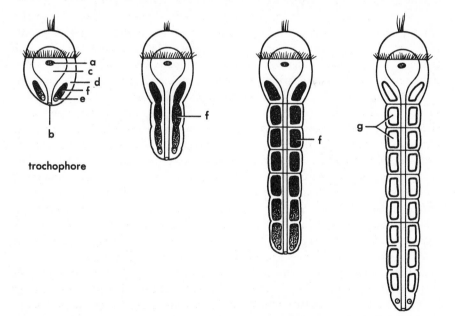

Fig. 3-15. Diagrammatic representation of the metamorphosis of a trochophore to a segmented worm. See text for details; a, mouth; b, anus; c, gut; d, blastocoel; e, the pair of cells that gives rise to mesoderm; f, mesoderm; g, coelomic pouches.

the transverse partitions between consecutive segmental pairs of pouches are the septa; the mid-dorsal and mid-ventral partitions separating the two members of a pair are called mesenteries.

The remainder of development involves the formation of various external and internal adult organ systems. The larva, which up until now may have remained free swimming (with the ciliated trochophore "head" pointing up), settles on the bottom, loses its crown of cilia, and begins life as a worm.

Since annelids are an enormously diverse group, it should come as no surprise that there is great variability in many details and even in major features of their development. Thus it is that the trochophore—which in itself is highly variable in appearance among polychaetes—is entirely missing among earthworms and their many fresh-water relatives (can you think of reasons why this should be the case?). But despite this variability, one fact stands out. The origin of the coelom from paired mesodermal pouches is a remarkably constant process. Our main expectation has therefore been confirmed: irrespective of the future fate of the septa—that is, whether they are retained in the adult—the embryo always begins by constructing a full set of them. It is therefore entirely possible that full septation was the ancestral annelid condition, and that locomotion in these ancestral forms was somewhat in the manner of that of an earthworm, at least to the extent that it depended on a hydrostatic skeleton of serially arranged liquid pouches.

There was also something *unexpected* about the embryology. When the coelom first develops there is formed a *pair* of compartments per segment, and not a single compartment as might have been anticipated. For the moment let us ignore this fact, although there is no denying that it may be of evolutionary significance (could it be that ancestral annelids had *two* rows of liquid pouches in their bodies rather than a single row?). Suffice it to say that in modern annelids the mesenteries are usually not retained in the adult. Even in an earthworm, which retains intact all of its septa, the mesenteries break down (in part) and the two coelomic compartments of each segment become confluent above and below the gut.

Where do we go from here? Fossil evidence from the Cambrian has told us little, other than that polychaetes of that period already had many of the features of their modern equivalents, and we inferred from this that they probably did not have a fully septated body cavity. From the embryological evidence we are now led to believe that incomplete septation is really a derived condition, and that the true ancestral annelids from Precambrian times might have had a fully compartmentalized coelom. We speculated earlier that the single most important factor that forced polychaetes to depart from the ancestral fully septated condition and to adopt instead an imperfectly or incompletely septated coelom might have been the advent of the arthropods. But what exactly was the interaction between ancestral annelids and the first arthropods, and why should this interaction have forced the annelids to decompartmentalize their body cavity? Let us speculate a bit.

Precambrian life

Suppose we were to make the following assumptions about Precambrian annelids: they were segmented elongate and flattened worms, crawling on the ocean floor, and feeding primarily on sediment. Although we cannot really justify these detailed assumptions in terms of evidence presented thus far, let us see whether they do not, in fact, make some sense.

First, is it reasonable to say that they were bottom dwellers? The very fact that they were worms would make it unreasonable to assume that they were anything else. If they had a compartmentalized coelom and crawled about somewhat in the manner of earthworms, it is hard to see how they could also have been effective swimmers. They might have had a free-swimming larva, perhaps even a trochophore no different from that of modern forms, but as adults it is more probable that they led a sedentary life. Even modern polychaetes constitute a distinctly bottom-dwelling group, and those forms like *Neanthes* that can swim rather well do so thanks to special adaptations such as parapodia that might, as we argued before, not have been present in ancestral forms.

Does it make sense that they led an exposed existence on the bottom, rather than living in tubes and burrows as did their later polychaete descendants? It is conceivable that, at the time annelids first evolved, the floor of the ocean was a reasonably "safe" place. We can be certain that there were no predators in existence of the types that were to make life hazardous for the polychaetes of Cambrian and subsequent times. An ocean without fish, without crustaceans, and without mollusks might be difficult to imagine, yet we know from the fossil record that this is the way things must have been. On the ocean floor there were probably sponges present, as well as perhaps flatworms (Platyhelminthes) and the first corals, but these would not have made life particularly dangerous for a bottom-crawling annelid. No matter what other unfamiliar animals might have existed at that time, it is highly doubtful that any of them were fast-moving hunters. Rapid locomotion is something that in the world of today is almost always associated with the possession of hard skeletons, but in the Precambrian there were not as yet animals with such skeletons in existence; this is one reason why Precambrian fossils are so scarce, for skeletal parts are the ones that are best fossilized. An exposed sluggish existence on the ocean floor was therefore a distinct possibility when the annelids first came into being. It might have been only later, when the annelids increased in number and kind, and when for the first time they experienced crowding and keen competition, that some of them became predaceous, forcing others into a more sheltered existence within burrows and tubes. And later still, when that formidable group, the arthropods, came into the picture, it was the sheltered forms that managed to survive, while those leading a more exposed existence became extinct. Arthropods might literally have eaten them out of existence. Incidentally, the reason we suspect that the earliest annelids were flattened is that this is a logical shape for a worm that crawls on the ocean floor (why do you suppose we think so?). It was only the later tube-dwelling and burrowing forms that acquired the cylindrical shape that nowadays we tend to associate with annelids. Parapodia, such as we find in *Neanthes* of today, or in polychaetes of the Burgess Shale, were probably not present in the flattened ancestral forms. The later sheltered forms might have been the first to adopt such parapodia, primarily as a means of setting up respiratory and feeding currents within the potentially stagnant confines of their hiding place. Once parapodial "paddles" had been perfected for this purpose, they could evidently also serve without substantial modification for locomotion outside the shelter (as they do in *Neanthes*). There was then no longer a need for retaining a hydrostatic skeleton like that of an earthworm, and the adult coelom became decompartmentalized. Actually, one need not assume that the ancestral flattened forms had no parapodia whatever. Perhaps they had incipient parapodia in the form of lateral projections or spines that might have helped them get a grip on the substrate as they crawled along. You will recall that locomotion in the earthworm is also dependent on a proper grip obtained with extrusible bristles.

Why should ancestral annelids have been sediment feeders? There are, of course, sediment feeders even among the polychaetes of today. *Arenicola*, you will recall, feeds on organic matter that it extracts from sand in its burrow. But where does the organic matter in ocean sand come from? A major source, and one that is likely to have been in existence even long before annelids first evolved, is that vast mixed population of tiny animals and plants in plankton. Plankton forms the bulk of living matter in the oceans. It is like a living blanket, spread through the surface waters of the seas. From the plankton above, to the ocean floor below, there is a continuous downward filtration of organic matter. Nowadays, organisms such as *Arenicola* that exploit organic sediment are by no means rare, and they include many animals from other phyla. But what about in Precambrian times? Once plankton became a dominant population, and an established source of organic sediment, might not annelids have been among the first pioneers that successfully colonized the ocean floor? And is it not logical that they should have fed on sediment, since this was the primary food source that the new environment had to offer? All they had to do was suck into their guts the very bottom ooze on which they crawled. As these annelids increased in number and became diversified, it is quite possible, as we reasoned before, that competitive pressures forced some of them to adopt shelters. But at first, during the early stages of expansion of the group, before things really became crowded, the way for an annelid to live if it was to feed on bottom ooze was obviously to crawl on the surface of it. There was no point in burrowing, since it was the surface layers that had the most to offer. Recall that even *Arenicola* derives its nourishment primarily from rich surface sand that trickles down the main shaft of its burrow. If one could somehow dive into the seas of the past, one might have reported, on seeing the Precambrian ocean floor during the early heyday of annelid evolution, "worm-tracks worm-tracks, everywhere. . . ."

There is one other thing that might be mentioned. We argued previously that at the time annelids first evolved, the ocean floor might have been rather barren and hence relatively safe. There is reason to believe that the plankton of that time might not at all have been so safe. There were already jellyfish in existence, and these must have been a hazard to anything alive drifting into their path. Living on the ocean floor was an effective way of avoiding them. Jellyfish might therefore have played an important part in having encouraged, as it were, the emigration from plankton and the colonization of new habitats like the ocean floor.

With all this speculation we have become a bit diverted from our central objective. We wanted to know whether ancestral annelids had the type of compartmentalized coelom that must have enabled them to crawl like earthworms. We have now succeeded in convincing ourselves that they might indeed have resembled crawling earthworms, except that they were flat and crawled on the ocean floor. What *you* should do next, before you read what follows, is to attempt to figure out how exactly such an annelid might have moved. Assume that it had a compartmentalized coelom, but take into consideration the flattened shape. Make certain also that the animal can do more than just crawl in a straight line. It must be able to turn. Also, don't forget that one might justifiably endow this flattened annelid with incipient parapodia in the form of some sort of lateral bristles or flaps. You will probably find that its movement could not have been quite like that of an earthworm. But there are variants of this type of locomotion that might have been possible, and that still depended on a compartmentalized hydrostatic skeleton.

There is something else you might wish to bear in mind. You will recall that in the annelid embryo the coelom arises as two parallel rows of segmental pouches. The possibility should therefore not be dismissed that ancestral annelids might have had two rows of coelomic pouches in their flattened adult bodies, rather than the single row possessed by a cylindrical earthworm. We raised this possibility before, but did not consider its implications. Might not the fact that the nephridia occur in pairs, rather than as single segmental units, be taken to suggest that ancestral annelids had two coelomic compartments per segment? Also—and this we did not emphasize before—the nerve cord of modern annelids, like that of the arthropods that arose from them, is really made up of two closely spaced parallel cords. Might this indicate that ancestral flattened annelids had two distinctly separate cords, one cord accompanying each row of coelomic compartments? Whatever assumptions you choose to favor, make certain you can justify them in terms of the adaptive demands of the particular types of locomotion you are designing.

Spriggina floundersi

A series of papers has appeared in the past few years describing a remarkable group of fossils from the Late Precambrian that were found in the Ediacara Hills of South Australia. These fossils are beautifully preserved, which is all the more remarkable since the animals were all essentially soft-bodied and lacked the skeletons and shells that are the usual prerequisites for proper fossilization. What makes these fossils so valuable is that they represent the oldest population of metazoan animals known. For the first time we can look back into the Precambrian and get a true idea of what the animals of that time were like. The most interesting thing to us is that the fossils date back to prearthropod times, but they do not antedate the advent of annelids. There is at least one unmistakably annelid worm present, and from this animal—*Spriggina floundersi*—we can finally learn something about the nature of annelids in the earlier days of their evolution, before they were forced into competition with arthropods and other later forms (Fig. 3–16).

Spriggina has some of the features that we had predicted for ancestral annelids. It is flattened, distinctly segmented, and must in all probability have been a bottom crawler. Along each side of its body there is a row of what could evidently be called parapodia. They are lateral projections terminating in single needlelike spines. Since they are not paddlelike in structure, it is doubtful that they could have been used effectively for swimming. Along the dorsal mid-line of the worm there is a conspicuous groove. This could indicate that the gut had become collapsed during fossilization. On each side of this groove the animal is distinctly segmented. Could this suggest that there were two rows of coelomic compartments, one on each side of the gut? There is obviously no way we can be certain of how exactly this worm crawled. There is no reason, however, why some speculation might not be in order. We leave this entirely up to you. Can you reconcile the hypothetical locomotory schemes that you postulated earlier with the known structural features of *Spriggina*? How might the muscles of this worm have been arranged? Would you expect the longitudinal musculature to have been arranged into dorsolateral and ventrolateral bundles as in *Neanthes*? In what way might the parapodia have been used? What might the nervous system

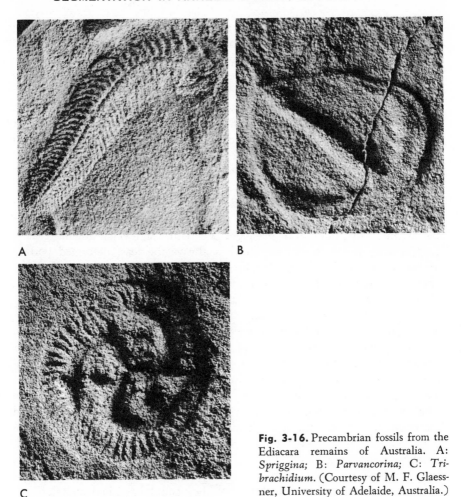

A

B

C

Fig. 3-16. Precambrian fossils from the Ediacara remains of Australia. A: *Spriggina*; B: *Parvancorina*; C: *Tribrachidium*. (Courtesy of M. F. Glaessner, University of Adelaide, Australia.)

have been like? Would you expect it to have consisted of two separate cords lying on each side of the gut (perhaps interconnected at the level of each segmental pair of ganglia), or might it already have resembled that of the modern annelids we studied, in that the two cords were mid-ventrally situated and virtually fused? Which of the two alternative arrangements would have provided a more economical way of supplying the necessary nervous circuitry? Answering this last question presupposes some understanding of the workings of the nervous system. With a bit of extra reading you should be able to diagram the basic nervous pathways that would be required to control the particular locomotory mechanism or mechanisms that you have devised.

Spriggina was by no means alone on the ocean floor of its day. Fossilized "worm" tracks, and even what appear to be burrows, are quite common among the Ediacara remains. Whether the tracks were indeed made by worms, and more specifically by annelid worms, is something of which we obviously cannot be sure. But it does seem certain that the ocean floor was already teeming with animals that crawled, and it is therefore possible that the annelids themselves were already at that time a diversified group. In fact, there is some reason to believe that *Spriggina* was in some ways a rather specialized form that had already departed from the presumed ancestral annelid condition. It might have been a predator rather than a sediment feeder. If, as we presume, the groove along its back is an indication of a collapsed gut, then it is more likely that the gut was filled with soft tissue-remains than that it was packed with sand. Also of interest is the fact that the horseshoe-shaped "head" might not have been as soft as the rest of the animal, but might have been encased within a skeletal shield. This is suggested by the fact that the head is always the least deformed portion of this fossil. Such a shield could have afforded some protection against enemies, but its primary function might have been to provide for a rigid place of insertion for special muscles used in feeding.

There were also some totally unwormlike animals that shared *Spriggina's* habitat. Two of these, *Parvancorina* and *Tribrachidium* (Fig. 3–16), we could never have predicted since they betray no affinities with any other animals known, either living or fossil. They apparently represent evolutionary lineages that were destined to become extinct before the Cambrian. These unexpected finds lead one to wonder whether we might have somewhat oversimplified things when we assumed that the first annelids had the ocean floor pretty much to themselves in the early days of their evolution. Who is to tell what other animal forms, wormlike or unwormlike, inhabited the bottom ooze when the annelids first came into being. In fact, one wonders from what particular group of animals the annelids might have arisen. It is our own feeling that they could have had ancestors not much different from some of the free-living flatworms (Platyhelminthes) that still exist in the world today. But this is another story, and one on which we shall not dwell here. Perhaps you might on your own try to spell out the type of transformations and innovations that would have had to take place in the hypothetical evolutionary transition from platyhelminth to annelid.

This is as far as we shall take our annelid story. We have by no means found the answers to all that we had initially wanted to know. Even our principal question—whether ancestral annelids had a compartmentalized coelom—has remained essentially unanswered. The embryological evidence presented can be considered suggestive at best. *Spriggina* did have some of the general features that we had predicted for ancestral annelids, but there is no way we can be certain of how exactly this animal moved, nor whether it did in fact possess a hydrostatic skeleton consisting of one or perhaps two rows of coelomic pouches. We are therefore not at all in a position to say categorically that ancestral annelids had a compartmentalized coelom, that this was the central feature of their segmentation, and that it repre- sented, first and foremost, an adaptation to a special type of locomotion. Nor can we therefore claim without reservation that the incomplete septa- tion of later polychaetes is a derived condition that evolved when these worms changed their locomotion and adopted shelters as a result of com- petitive pressures to which the ancestral forms had not been exposed. We also cannot be sure that earthworms are direct descendants of certain of these ancestral forms that escaped the new pressures by emigrating at an early time from the seas, and that this is why earthworms retained in essentially unchanged condition the original septate body plan. The only thing we can say with some degree of satisfaction is that we have uncovered no evidence that is in obvious contradiction to our postulated ideas. Admittedly this is a far cry from saying that the evidence speaks unmistakably in their favor. Our hypothesis can at best be claimed to hold the field by default. We, at any rate, can think of no better one with which to replace it. Perhaps you can. You might disagree with some of our reasoning, and you might feel that we have overlooked some important lines of evidence.

SEGMENTATION IN ARTHROPODS

Segmentation is not necessarily the most obvious characteristic of an arthropod. If one compares an earthworm and a mosquito, one quickly recognizes the segmental features of the worm, and points out the annula- tions of the body wall, the internal septa, and the serially repeated ganglia, nephridia, and segmental blood vessels. But about the mosquito, one is first likely to notice such things as a body divided into head, thorax, and abdomen, the presence of legs and wings, and a hard exoskeleton. In other words, at first glance the dissimilarities between the two forms are likely to be more conspicuous than the similarities. Only if pressed further to look specifically for those characters that the two forms have in common is one likely to notice that the mosquito is also in some ways segmented. One would then point out the abdominal segments and their associated mus- culature (Fig. 1–13B), and the serially arranged ganglia that make up the ventral nerve cord (Fig. 1–19), but that is about all. True, the mosquito has some serially repeated features of its own, such as the three pairs of legs, the spiracles, and the alary muscles of the heart (Fig. 1–12A), but neither the head nor the thorax betray any obvious outer signs of segmentation, and nowhere in the animal are there to be found the septa, paired nephridia, and segmental blood vessels that are so characteristic of an earthworm.

Evidently, an arthropod such as a mosquito shows some rather radical departures from the annelid body plan. The significant thing about segmentation in arthropods, then, is not so much the fact that it occurs. Arthropods are, after all, presumed to stem from annelids, and segmentation is an important part of their evolutionary heritage. The remarkable thing is the long way that arthropods have gone toward the suppression of those segmental features that they have inherited from annelids. If we are to explain segmentation in arthropods we must therefore find evolutionary justifications for this suppression. What are the structural and functional innovations that set arthropods apart from their annelid ancestors? And why should the evolution of these innovations have led to a concurrent suppression of segmentation?

The evolutionary transition from annelid to arthropod is not written out in the fossil record. When arthropods first appear among fossils of the Cambrian they present themselves as a *fait accompli*. Even the earliest known trilobites are already full-fledged arthropods in every sense of the word. There are no forms known, either living or fossil, that we can be certain represent intermediates between annelids and arthropods. If we want to reconstruct the early evolution of arthropods, we are therefore forced again to rely on speculation and on whatever indirect evidence may be obtainable.

Let us do the following. Let us first try to establish those fundamental characteristics of arthropods that are distinctly arthropodan. In other words, let us pinpoint those major features that arthropods have acquired on their own and do not share with annelids. Then, taking these features for granted, and without questioning how exactly they might have evolved, let us see if we can predict what the remainder of the arthropod body *ought* to be like. We have already done something comparable with the earthworm. You will recall that first we focused attention on the compartmentalized coelom and on the segmental arrangement of musculature and ganglia, and then we went on to predict the existence of a closed circulatory system and the presence of serially repeated excretory organs.

The two outstanding characteristics of arthropods not shared with annelids are the possession of a hard exoskeleton and the possession of legs. The very fact that arthropods have legs emphasizes that their locomotion is mechanically entirely different from what it is in annelids. Think of a centipede walking, and contrast this with an earthworm. Changes in body girth, such as are so essential for the moving earthworm, become totally superfluous for an animal that pushes itself forward by means of legs. Even *Neanthes*, you will recall, which when crawling relies on its parapodia, shows no changes in body girth comparable to those of an earthworm, and it has, in fact, a body cuticle that prevents such changes from taking place. It also lacks perfect septa, so that even if it had no cuticle, it would still be incapable of crawling like an earthworm. What *Neanthes* tells us is that if locomotion depends on appendages, then there is no reason why the body wall cannot be skeletized, and if the body wall is skeletized, then there is no reason why the coelom need remain compartmented. Now, in arthropods, there are legs present, and there is also an exoskeleton. Hence, the first thing we would venture to predict is that arthropods have done away with coelom compartmentalization since they have no need for an internal hydrostatic skeleton. There should be no septa inside their bodies. We already know that this is so in mosquitoes, but it is also true for arthropods in general.

What happens during the embryological development of an arthropod? Are there formed first, as in annelids, segmental pairs of mesodermal pouches that by gradual enlargement come to fill the blastocoel, and is the open body cavity of an arthropod formed by the subsequent coalescence of these meso-dermal pouches as a result of a breakdown of the septae between them? Arthropods do indeed form segmental mesodermal pouches early in their embryology, but the development of the pouches is brought to a halt at a much earlier stage than in annelids. In an arthropod, the coelomic pouches never become large enough to fill the blastocoel. In fact, the body cavity of the adult arthropod *is* the blastocoel. In this respect an arthropod differs fundamentally from an annelid. One may wonder why the arthropod embryo has not altogether eliminated the building of coelomic pouches if these pouches are not to be put to a later postembryonic use. Actually, the cellular walls of the pouches, which as you may recall constitute the so-called mesodermal tissue, are not at all superfluous, and they give rise in the developing arthropod to many of the same tissues and organs that they also form in an annelid: for example, the musculature of the body wall and gut, the blood vessels, and the gonads. In other words, what the arthropod has suppressed is not mesoderm formation itself, but only the full expansion of the coelomic cavities. As development proceeds, even the incipient coelomic cavities of the arthropod embryo eventually disappear almost in their entirety. Only a few of them are retained, but these are put to a use not at all related to locomotion. The cavities within the adult gonads, for instance, can be traced back to coelomic spaces of the embryo.

Once we know that arthropods have an open body cavity, other fea-tures of their anatomy and physiology lend themselves to prediction. Does it not make sense that the fluid of the body cavity should serve in the capacity of blood? In the absence of internal partitions there is nothing to oppose the flow of materials from one part of the organism to another via the fluid in the body cavity. The term hemocoele (literally, blood cavity) used for the body cavity of an arthropod is therefore sensible. We speak of the circulatory system of an arthropod as being an open system. Major vessels are kept to a minimum, and capillaries are completely absent. In the mosquito, the single dorsal blood vessel is all that remains of the elaborate ancestral annelid vascular system. It communicates directly with the body cavity, and through its contraction effects a stirring of the blood. Such a simple system is evidently adequate for an animal whose blood serves primarily for the distribution of nutrients and has no respiratory function. But in those arthropods that lack a tracheal system and do distribute oxygen by way of the blood, there are sometimes present, in addition to the dorsal vessel, a series of other vessels radiating to various portions of the body. This is the case in a crayfish. The circulatory system of this animal is no less an open one than that of the mosquito, since the various vessels do not communicate with each other by capillaries, but open directly into the body cavity. But circulation is evidently much more precisely directed in an animal that channels its blood through a multiplicity of vessels than it is in the mosquito. For the crayfish, the retention of an elaborate duct system is a matter of some importance, since it enables the animal to maintain separate pathways for the deoxygenated and oxygenated blood flowing to and from the gills (Fig. 2–11). Insects, by virtue of their tracheal system, were able to carry the reduction of their blood-vessel system to an extreme.

The fact that arthropods have an open body cavity can also lead us to predict that they need not possess an excretory system identical to that of their annelid ancestors. According to our earlier reasoning, serially repeated nephridia are justified in annelids because these animals face the problem of evacuating wastes from individually sealed coelomic compartments. Once the body cavity is no longer compartmentalized, one can expect a more consolidated excretory system to prevail—at least there would seem to be no need for retaining a full complement of segmental units. You will recall that among annelids there sometimes has occurred a reduction in the number of nephridia in such forms as *Arenicola,* which have a partly decompartmentalized coelom. In arthropods, there exist excretory organs of diverse types. Some of these, such as the Malpighian tubules of insects, are complete innovations and bear no relation whatever to the ancestral annelid nephridia. But others, judging from the similarity of their embryological origin to that of nephridia, represent mere modified versions of the annelid organs. Arthropods, however, never retain a full multisegmental set of such modified nephridia. In scorpions, for instance, there are two excretory organs called coxal glands, which open at the base of a pair of legs, and which are considered to be modified nephridia. So are the two excretory organs of a crayfish, called antennal glands, which open at the base of the antennae (Fig. 3–17). In arthropods, the acquisition of an unpartitioned body cavity by the early representatives of the group evidently opened the way for the adoption of different alternative types of excretory systems, and several such alternatives were indeed preserved by a variety of the descendent evolutionary lineages.

We have now examined some of those features of annelids that have

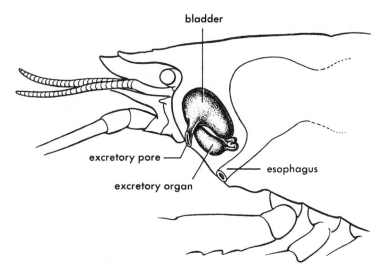

Fig. 3-17. Front end of a crayfish, showing its left excretory apparatus. (From Griffin, *Animal Structure and Function*, Holt, Rinehart and Winston, Inc.)

been profoundly modified in arthropods. Let us next look at those segmental characteristics that have been preserved with relatively little change. In most arthropods there is at least one portion of the body where the exoskeleton maintains a distinct segmentation. In the mosquito it is the abdomen. In a centipede it is most of the body. In a crayfish it is the "tail." By contrast, other portions of the body have had their segments partially or completely fused. Such is the case with the head of a centipede, the head and thorax of an insect, and the cephalothorax of a crayfish. Sometimes the fusion of segments is so complete in a given region that it is no longer possible to determine the exact segmental make-up of that region. With the insect head, for instance, we can be fairly certain that it consists of at least three segments, but we do not know precisely how many additional segments might have gone into its composition. There is obvious adaptive significance to the possession of body regions in which segments have become consolidated. The fused group of segments that forms the cranial shell of an insect or a centipede provides the animal with a protective enclosure for its brain, and at the same time offers a firm place of attachment for the muscles that operate the mouth parts. Similarly, the thorax, whose three segments are rigidly fused in most winged insects, provides an appropriately firm skeletal box for the powerful musculature of wings and legs. But there is also adaptive significance to the fact that in some body regions a clear segmentation has been preserved. Instead of being fused, the segments maintain their individuality and are hinged to each other by thin and flexible membranes. Such membranes provide for an intersegmental mobility without which the animal would be handicapped in a variety of ways. Think of a centipede dashing about, bending and turning as it circumvents obstacles in its path, and think of the predicament the animal would face if its body were inflexible. The segmented tail of crayfish, which is also flexible, can be flung forward beneath the body, and is used to propel the animal backward. In an insect, the retention of intersegmental membranes in the abdomen is not to be viewed strictly as an adaptation to locomotion, but, as we mentioned earlier, as a means of providing the animal with a distensible housing for its viscera (in addition to other functions). Wherever segments have failed to fuse, and where consequently a certain degree of intersegmental mobility is retained, there are muscles present that effect this mobility. These muscles, which consist mostly of longitudinal intersegmental fibers (Fig. 1–13B), are a carry-over of the longitudinal musculature of the ancestral annelid's body wall. The circular musculature of the annelid has been appropriated in the arthropod for the performance of a new task—that of moving the legs. It is clear, then, that although in arthropods the tendency to suppress segmentation has gone so far as to involve virtual fusion of groups of segments, there are usually present in arthropods, for adaptive reasons that differ in various forms, regions of the body in which the exoskeleton preserves a distinct segmentation.

There is one additional annelid feature that was adopted intact, or essentially intact, by arthropods. This is the nervous system. In arthropods, as in annelids, the central nervous system consists of a brain and a ventral chain of ganglia. In annelids we justified the possession of such a nerve cord in term of the adaptive demands of their special locomotion. We argued that it makes sense for an earthworm to have its ganglia arranged segmentally, because the musculature of the body wall is also segmented, at least in the sense that the muscles of the various segments operate as functional units. In arthropods, locomotion involves the use of legs, and these legs are also distributed segmentally. Hence, it is only to be expected that the original segmental arrangement of the ganglia has been preserved, particularly since the leg muscles innervated by these ganglia apparently correspond to the original circular body muscles already similarly innervated in annelid progenitors. You may wonder why a mosquito preserves segmental ganglia in the abdomen, where there are no legs. The abdomen, however, does possess muscles of its own, and these muscles, as we saw, are arranged into units that stretch from segment to segment. It therefore makes good sense that there should be a series of abdominal ganglia whose distribution parallels that of the segmentally arranged muscles they control. Thus, in arthropods, there is a dual reason for the retention of an essentially annelid central nervous system: the possession of segmental appendages, and the maintenance of a segmentally arranged musculature of the body wall. Actually, even as regards the nervous system, there has been a tendency among many arthropods to depart from the primitive segmental annelid pattern. Most often this manifests itself in a fusion of ganglia from two or more consecutive segments. Thus, for instance, in an insect, the first ganglion of the ventral nerve cord is supposedly a composite ganglion made up of ganglia from three segments. An extreme case of ganglion consolidation is illustrated by a relative of the mosquito, the housefly, in which all abdominal and thoracic ganglia have become fused into a single giant ganglion situated in the thorax.

We mentioned earlier that the two major characteristics that distinguish arthropods from annelids are the possession of legs and the possession of an exoskeleton. We have now seen that almost everything else about the body plan of an arthropod makes good sense when viewed in the light of these two major characteristics. What we have been ignoring all along is how the legs and the exoskeleton might have evolved in the first place. We really cannot answer this in any precise detail because there is no fossil evidence. It seems reasonable, however, that the acquisition of legs antedated the evolution of an exoskeleton. Before the body could be hardened, there must have been appendages present on which the animal could rely for lomotion. At first these legs were probably no more than short lobes. It was only later that they increased in length, when the possession of an exoskeleton in the legs made an increase in length mechanically feasible. We may there-fore picture the early intermediates between annelids and arthropods as having been elongate wormlike forms with segmental pairs of stubby legs along the length of their bodies. The next major advance was the acquisition of an exoskeleton, perhaps first around the body itself, and only later around the appendages. The appendages increased in length, became jointed, and eventually a greater or lesser number of them became specialized for func-tions other than locomotion. The claws of a lobster, the fangs of a spider, and the mouth parts of a mosquito—all these are modified segmental append-ages. The enormous diversity that arthropods eventually were to achieve is perhaps attributable, more than to anything else, to the phenomenal versatility of their appendages.

There is a remarkable group of animals, still living, and known from fossils as ancient as the Burgess Shale, that have an astounding resemblance to what one might have expected the evolutionary intermediates between arthropods and annelids to have been like. These animals, the so-called Onychophora (*Peripatus* and its relatives), have a soft wormlike body and a full set of short walking legs (Figs. 3–13, 3–18). There are, however, unique features about the anatomy of the Onychophora that suggest that they represent a lone offshoot of the Annelida not at all closely related to the particular lineage that was to give rise to arthropods. Thus, all we can say about Onychophora is that they are similar—perhaps misleadingly so—

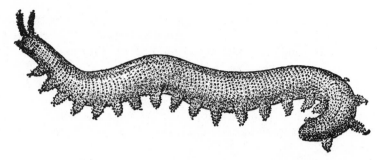

Fig. 3-18. *Peripatus.* (From Hegner and Stiles, *College Zoology,* The Macmillan Company.)

to hypothetical arthropod progenitors. One wonders how exactly the arthropod appendages got their evolutionary start. It has been suggested that they arose from annelid parapodia, but there has been a recent tendency to deny this possibility. However, these arguments all took place before the discovery of *Spriggina.* This unusual worm has certain striking similarities to some of the early trilobites, and to us it no longer seems farfetched to presume that parapodia such as those of *Spriggina* might have been the forerunners of arthropod legs. We shall not pursue this question any further, and we shall abandon our discussion of early arthropod evolution at this point, but there is no reason why you could not pursue this line of inquiry on your own.

In retrospect, looking over this chapter, we find that there are only very few questions for which we have found satisfactory answers. This is not to say that all the remaining questions are unanswerable, although undoubtedly many of them are. We have neither investigated all available lines of evidence, nor have we exploited to the limit those lines that we did pursue. Our purpose was solely to begin an exploration. It was not our intent to make an exhaustive search, nor did we believe that the particular questions we asked were especially profound and fundamental ones. Chances are that if you asked biologists about the evolutionary justification of segmentation in annelids, they would tell you that they don't know or that they don't care. Some might offer hypotheses quite different from our own. Our point in this chapter was simply to look into a given adaptation, and to think of it *in the perspective of its evolutionary past.* We could have done this with any biological adaptation. We need not have chosen, as we did, an adaptive feature of a whole organism or group of organisms. We could just as well have taken a single molecule, and asked how that particular molecule evolved to achieve the adaptive fitness by which we know it today. Our claim is that such inquiries are never a waste of time. They are a basic part of biological thinking. True, to pursue such inquiries may cause more questions to be raised than are actually answered. But is this not a good thing?

SUGGESTED READING LIST

BUCHSBAUM, R., 1948. *Animals without backbones.* Chicago: University of Chicago Press.

GLAESSNER, M. F., "Pre-Cambrian animals," *Scientific American,* March 1961, pp. 72–78.

KUMMEL, B., 1961. *History of the earth.* San Francisco: W. H. Freeman and Company.

RAMSAY, J. A., 1952. *A physiological approach to the lower invertebrates.* New York: Cambridge University Press.

ROMER, A. S., 1941. *Man and the vertebrates.* Chicago: University of Chicago Press.

WELLS, G. P., "The life of the lugworm," *New Biology,* Vol. 22 (1957), pp. 39–55.

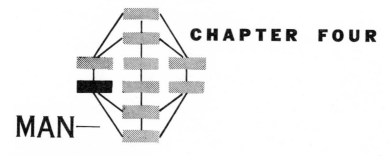

CHAPTER FOUR

MAN—

A SPECIAL

CASE?

Every species, animal or plant, has its own special features. So much has been written about man and his own claim to distinctiveness that we need not elaborate the point here. Man has an extraordinarily versatile hand and a highly developed brain to direct it. This, in short, is what makes him unique.

Perhaps nothing is more startling to us as humans than our own success. Despite a relatively low reproductive potential, we have spread over this earth like bacteria in a Petri dish. A few millenia ago we numbered in the thousands; now we are approaching the four billion mark. We have constructed great civilizations. We have an extraordinary ability to learn; we teach our children, and pass onto them the recorded experiences of previous generations. We can survive anywhere on earth. We go to the poles, move under water in submarines, climb the highest mountains, tunnel underground, and penetrate the atmosphere. Now we are entering outer space, and we have scheduled foreseeable trips to other planets. We have altered major regions of the earth; we have dredged, drained, and plowed. We manufacture antibiotics and insecticides, and can in other ways combat species that threaten us. In brief, we are uniquely aware of our adaptive shortcomings, and we have learned to alter the environment to suit us, or to transport intact portions of our environment into otherwise uninhabitable places.

Judging from our success in the past, we tend to feel that our future is assured. But as biologists we should be well aware of the potentially transient nature of adaptive success. While it seems unlikely that we are on the verge of extinction, it does seem appropriate to interject a note of caution into what might otherwise be an overly optimistic outlook on our future.

We are increasing in enormous numbers. Within the next 50 years, the population of the earth will double. We may be the only species in which the living of today outnumber all the dead of the past. The population "explosion" is a *real* explosion, and it is entirely unlikely that we will have learned to colonize other planets in time to accommodate a terrestrial population in need of mass emigration. Emigration, at any rate, is not the solution. Even to maintain our population at the present level would require a daily departure of rockets with a total human payload of 50 million tons!

We are draining our resources at an unprecedented rate. Again, it seems doubtful that alternative resources can be found at a rate commensurate with the depletion of existing ones.

And finally, for the first time in our history, waste products—including atomic wastes—are becoming a major threat. Not even the best radiation geneticist in the world can gauge with absolute precision the long-range biological effects of an atmosphere that is being increasingly polluted with radioactivity.

As biologists, we can only point to these problems and to their inherent dangers. What is done to solve them depends on the role we choose to play as citizens.

SUGGESTED READING LIST

OSBORN, F., 1948. *Our plundered planet.* Boston: Little, Brown.
Scientific American, "The human species," September 1960 (entire issue).
THOMAS, W. L., JR. (ed.), 1958. *Man's role in changing the face of the earth.* Chicago: University of Chicago Press.
VOGT, W., 1948. *Road to survival.* New York: Sloan.
WALLACE, B., and DOBZHANSKY, TH., 1959. *Radiation, genes, and man.* New York: Holt, Rinehart and Winston, Inc.

INDEX

132